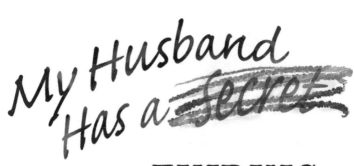

FINDING
HEALING

for the
Betrayal of sexual
addiction

MOLLY ANN MILLER

"All suffering contains gifts.
And sex addiction is no different."
—Dr. Patrick Carnes[1]

Beacon Hill Press of Kansas City
Kansas City, Missouri

Copyright 2005
by Molly Ann Miller and Beacon Hill Press of Kansas City

ISBN: 083-412-1840

Printed in the
United States of America

Cover Design: Darlene Filley

All Scripture quotations not otherwise designated are from *The Holy Bible, New International Version*® (NIV®). Copyright © 1973, 1978, 1984 by International Bible Society. Used by permission of Zondervan Publishing House. All rights reserved.

Library of Congress Cataloging-in-Publication Data
[to come]

10   9   8   7   6   5   4   3   2   1

DEDICATED

To my teachers:

Dr. Patrick Carnes, who taught me the truth about addiction,

Roger Thoman, who taught me to listen,

Cec Murphey, who taught me to write,

My husband,
whose honesty about his addiction
taught me to accept and love myself.

And my children,
who love both of us unconditionally,
and courageously shared their stories.

CONTENTS

INTRODUCTION

MY NAME IS NOT MOLLY. I could be your neighbor, your pastor's wife, your child's schoolteacher, or your close friend, and I probably am. Sex addiction is now an epidemic, and the church is no exception. "Sex is the fastest growing addiction in this country. And it is, I believe," writes Marnie Feree, who treats female sex addicts, "the addiction of choice among Christians . . . It is an incredible problem."[1]

Mark Laaser writes, "It's abundantly clear that sexual addiction does not discriminate with respect to gender."[2] I've endeavored to write without gender qualifications when possible.

Fifteen years ago my husband disclosed his secret—he'd been a sex addict for 19 years—our entire marriage. I struggled through the pain of betrayal the first year, sharing with a counselor and only one friend—an unfair burden that she bore with God-sized portions of grace. It would be 10 years before I would meet the wives of other sex addicts.

This is the story of the struggles of my own heart and what would have helped me. I encourage you to read the clinical books on this subject because mercy grows with understanding.

There's a lovely garden on the path ahead. Jesus is there to bind up our broken hearts. The depth of our pain is meant to enlarge our hearts to experience the heights of His love. His hands are qualified to offer us joy and comfort because they are pierced. Since He was betrayed by a kiss, He knows *exactly* how we feel.

The days ahead will not all be pleasant. Trust and fidelity have been destroyed and vows broken. You may think the battle is for your marriage, but that is just a skirmish. As John Eldredge reminds the Church, "The battle is for our hearts."[3] Whether your relationship survives—or not—you can be victorious in the battle for your heart. You can live fully as God intended as your true self is freed from the faulty beliefs that imprison you. You can reflect God's glory.

The truth is in the light at last,
A truth so strong, it's robbed your past,
Every memory is now debated,
In light of the truth his confession created.

New losses assault your mind each day,
It feels like sorrow is here to stay.
And the only way to healthy grieving
Is to feel the feelings of bereaving.

It was just an illusion, a deception, a lie,
The fairy tale you lived must die.
The new reality you must embrace
Is full of pain, shame, disgrace.

But God is beckoning anew,
He'll pick you up and carry you.
He says he died for sin and shame,
The abundant life is yours to claim.

You ask me how this can be so?
I walked your path not long ago.
That path is strewn with pain and tears
Rejection, sorrow, lonely fears.

I call to you from up the path:
"There's joy ahead; you will laugh!
God pruned away what was stunted,
To give me what I always wanted."

Russell Willingham said, "What is a wife to do? Grieve well, set boundaries and face herself . . . let God and others love her back to wholeness."[4]

My prayer is that you will feel understood, comforted, and encouraged. You are *not* alone.

With hope,
Molly Ann Miller

YOU ARE NOT ALONE

"The only person who feels greater shame than the sex addict himself is often the addict's wife . . . surely if she were 'woman enough,' her man would not need to 'have his needs met' elsewhere. This line of thinking is a cruel lie, but it places innumerable women under a tremendous burden of guilt, and prevents them from seeking the counsel and support they so badly need."
—Steve Arterburn[1]

MY EYES DARTED NERVOUSLY AROUND THE circle. I longed to share the story I'd guarded for 10 years, desperate for a safe place to release it. Yet I dreaded to speak the words already constricting my throat: prostitutes, lies, and betrayal.

The facilitator, Carol, began the meeting, and my stomach felt queasy. Others shifted in their chairs. She read the rules: the most important one to me was that everything shared was strictly confidential. No names or information were to be repeated, not even to our husbands. We went around the room and shared our first names. I couldn't remember a single one.

Books were opened with stories of recovery and hope written by others who had experienced healing. Carol began reading. After each paragraph we were welcome to comment.

Sandy spoke up first. She introduced herself as a missionary. A recorded message on her husband's cell phone had exposed his affair. The mission board requested they return home immediately. Sandy withdrew her three children from school. Unable to explain to her confused children, she watched tearfully as they were separated from their closest friends.

Relationships with other missionary wives became awkward;

how truthful could she be and remain a respectful wife? Her isolation increased, as did her anger toward her husband. A week later she sat on a plane, feeling more alone than ever next to the man who betrayed her.

"Did I go to language school for a year, raise support for another year, and then move my family halfway around the world for *this*? God has failed me. I am really angry with Him right now."

Tears ran down her cheeks, and I wished my compassion could wipe them away. I was surprised at the depth of Sandy's pain. I came to this meeting assuming my pain would be the greatest. Here was someone who had lost far more than I had.

My pain wrapped itself around me like chains, choking what little energy I had. Waves of self-pity assailed me. I thought I had a right to feel sorry for myself, but Sandy's story stirred my doubt.

Lucy shared next. Her husband was addicted to pornography. I strained to hear her words as she told of long lapses in their sexual relationship. She'd tried to fill the emptiness in her heart with food, but the comfort she searched for backfired. Her tight clothing constantly reminded her she was only making things worse. "I hope I'm not responsible for it—you know—his addiction." Her downcast eyes finally looked up.

Reassuring looks comforted Lucy. Several of us were overweight. Chocolate obsessed my mind when painful thoughts tortured me, and I also felt undesirable. *I wonder if everyone here feels the same.*

This group was going to be good for me. Only two women had shared, and I already felt something changing inside me. Before coming to this meeting I'd felt isolated. As my gaze traveled around the room, I knew I was just like the others. They had suffered—some even more than I, and I knew I wasn't alone. The sum of my resources over the past 10 years was one book on the subject written for women, a workshop, and general recovery groups at my church. This was the first support group I found solely devoted to spouses of sex addicts.

I came out of my reverie as Valerie began to speak. She had

often wondered why they always seemed to be financially strapped. One day the phone company called about an enormous unpaid bill. Assuming it was a mistake, she asked her husband to check on it. When she brought it to his attention, he stammered. As he made excuses, her heart beat faster, fear rising within her. He broke down, confessing his shameful addiction to phone sex. Valerie's face reddened and her jaw tightened as she related how hard she worked while he financially sabotaged their marriage. "But that is nothing compared to the emotional sabotage I feel!"

Tina was young; in fact, she had just returned to college. "My counselor thought I should join this group. I was married to a sex addict for a year. He didn't think anything was wrong with his addiction. Our divorce was final last month. I wanted to put the past behind me, but my counselor said that I chose an addict because of my codependency issues. I'm likely to repeat the pattern if I don't deal with it, so here I am. I never want to go through anything like that again. I'm relieved something good can come out of what feels like a failure."

Jennifer described how her husband's attention seemed diverted when an attractive woman passed by. Curious glances gave way to lustful stares, held too long to be innocent. Occasionally, women smiled coyly back, and she felt anger rise within her. Was she imagining it? No. She admitted she even stopped talking when his eyes wandered from her face to gawk, waiting for the interruption to pass. If she said something, wouldn't it hurt their relationship more? One day she found a pile of magazines hidden under the couch. She was horrified as she thumbed through the pornography.

Her anger grew, empowering her to confront him as he walked through the door. His denial fueled her anger, strengthening her resolve for the truth. He finally admitted how ashamed he felt, and meekly accepted responsibility for his behavior. Her relief came when he agreed to counseling. She already noticed a change.

Denise told of countless nights when her husband worked in

front of the computer long after she was in bed. One day she checked the memory log. More than 100 porn sites appeared. Something was desperately wrong. Just reading the names made her feel dirty. "My greatest fear is that my son will model my husband's behavior." I realized the danger for my own boys. Her story brought many sighs. Apparently on-line pornography was a common problem.

In a flat voice, Linda described her husband's emotional affairs. He gained a feeling of importance from relationships with women who were overly-friendly. While he'd gotten his needs met elsewhere, she'd been lonely and unfulfilled. "It's been hard to identify exactly what's wrong, since he seems friendly and caring." But too often uneasiness washed over her when he was attentive to other women in social situations. "I was tempted too . . ." Her voice cracked and then tears rolled down her cheeks. "But I wanted to be loyal to him. This is so unfair!" Several other women wiped tears from their eyes.

So far no one had shared anything as awful as my husband had done. Was I still going to feel alone?

Sarah's husband was in jail, arrested for soliciting a prostitute. He had hidden two prior offenses from her. The first time she learned about his sexual misconduct was when he called her from jail. One phone call—and her life was shattered. "When our friends ask where he is, I don't know what to say. I'm sure he'll lose his job." How would she survive financially? She was so hurt that she didn't even want to see him, but their young children missed him terribly.

Even the heartbreaking behavior of my husband couldn't help me imagine this kind of shock. Sarah's identity had been publicly undermined. Not only did she bear the humiliation of her husband's arrest, but she was suffering the enormous rejection his unfaithfulness caused. I ached for her.

Sharon had been weeping quietly throughout the meeting. I doubted she would share, but she cleared her throat and my eyes turned toward her. Holding a tissue to her eyes, she told of her husband's attraction to the same sex. "He struggled with homosexuality years ago, but now it's returned. I wish I had *your* problems," she said. "I'm so ashamed my husband wants another *man* instead of me." She buried her face in her hands and sobbed. Her grief was reflected in stricken faces around the table.

I felt a deep kinship with this woman that I didn't anticipate. We'd both been betrayed, our hearts were broken, and it didn't matter what caused it.

It was finally my turn to share. In the last 10 years I'd told only a few of my closest friends about Timothy's addiction. My palms grew moist, and my stomach churned. The room grew quiet.

chapter 2

DISCLOSURE

ONE MORNING I NOTICED TEARS in my husband's eyes. I asked him what was wrong, and he told me he was just feeling emotional.

I thought, *The responsibilities of his business sure are hard on him.*

That morning our pastor called. "Molly, can you come to my office?"

I became uneasy when he wouldn't discuss anything over the phone. As I arrived, the secretary waved me in. When I opened the door, I saw Timothy sitting there. *Why isn't he at work?* I could see his hands tapping the arm of the chair—a sure sign to me of his nervousness. Our eyes met, and I sensed his fear. The pastor invited me to take the other chair.

"Timothy has something to tell you."

I mechanically turned toward him. *What's going on? Is he in some kind of trouble? Maybe with the law?* I searched both their faces for clues. They avoided eye contact. The atmosphere was so tense I could hardly breathe.

Timothy faced me but kept looking at his hands. "I've led a double life." He rocked back and forth slightly in his chair. "I've been unfaithful to you our whole marriage."

I blinked. *Unfaithful? My husband?* I opened my mouth but no words came out.

"I started going to X-rated movies not long after we got married. Then I went to adult bookstores."

"I had no idea—"

"Eventually I went to massage parlors and topless bars."

I went numb. I could hardly believe what I was hearing.

"I thought each time would be the last." His voice cracked

14

and I instinctively put my hand on his. He took his handkerchief out of his back pocket. "There's—there's more."

More? How much more could there be?

"Then I started going to prostitutes. Each time I'd vow never to go back. But I did—I kept going back."

Was I really at our church, listening to my husband say he'd been going to prostitutes?

"That's why I'm being honest with you now. I've contracted genital herpes. I was crying this morning because I found out my test results from the health department."

"Oh, Timothy!"

"I don't want you to get it."

We were both crying now. *I don't want herpes either!*

"I'm sure this is hard for you to hear, but I want to be honest with you from now on. That's why I'm telling you all this in front of our pastor. I want to be accountable. I'm tired of lying to you."

He squeezed my hands as if begging for mercy. His breathing was shallow and fast. "I'll leave if you want me to. I wouldn't blame you."

Do I want him to leave? We have six children. Until three minutes ago I thought we had a great marriage! Am I foolish to let him stay? Would it help him change if I asked him to leave?

His sad eyes searched my face. "Do you think you'll ever be able to forgive me?" His face contorted with sorrow and the sound of his sobs filled the small office.

Compassion overwhelmed me. "Yes, I forgive you."

Timothy had an addiction. We didn't understand that until we started counseling. They gave it a label: *sexual addiction.* He started attending Sexaholics Anonymous (SA) meetings every week. We read books on sex addiction, communication, and intimacy. I cried every single day that year, and grieved my loss of fidelity. He listened, cried with me, and apologized repeatedly. When I forgave him the first time, I didn't realize it would be a choice I would have to make countless times, and it would never get easier.

After eight months our counselor pronounced Timothy healed, but he continued to attend SA. We abstained from sex for six months, waiting for the results of his second HIV test. When the results came back negative, we renewed our vows and promised each other honesty—not perfection. We had learned that honesty was the price of unconditional love. Our new goal was unity—not happiness. We had to share all of ourselves—not only the parts we thought were acceptable—to end the shame and isolation.

The following years we enjoyed a deeper intimacy than we'd ever known. We were open with each other and trust slowly returned. We joined a church that focused on recovery from addictions. We went to weekly groups to help us recognize our feelings and express them responsibly. We learned that no one can meet all of our needs; only relationship with God can do that.

Our marriage was going well. Our oldest kids were teenagers. We had challenges with them I never thought we'd face in our home: drugs, lying, running away, and premarital sex. However, the biggest trauma came when our son's ex-girlfriend committed suicide—in our house. We all got counseling, but Timothy remained upset. He couldn't concentrate on his business, so we struggled financially.

Six months later we moved into a new house. I thought everything was fine, but I was wrong.

My husband got an offer to sell his demanding business. I was excited about more family time as we moved to a rural community. But when Timothy arrived home from his new job, he settled into his recliner with a book. One book followed another. After a few weeks I realized Timothy had changed. I don't know when it started, but he had withdrawn from me emotionally. We talked less, and when we did, he was so defensive the conversation ended with me in tears. We had experienced intimacy, and I was not willing to give it up. He seemed depressed, so I urged him to get counseling. His withdrawal caused feelings of loneliness and rejection for me, tapping into the pain of his unfaithfulness.

We were new in the community, and my husband was emotionally absent. I felt completely alone. Our relationship became so hurtful that I prayed he would die. When I heard his car drive up to the house I was sorry he was still alive, knowing the pain of rejection his arrival would bring. We went on like that for nine months—I finally told him we couldn't live together any longer. That spurred him into talking to our pastor who referred him to a counseling center.

I noticed an improvement right away. After a few weeks he invited me out on a date and took half the day off from work. I was excited that our relationship had turned a corner. I put on my favorite dress and we headed downtown. "Where are we going?" He wanted to surprise me, and I thought the intrigue was romantic. We pulled into the parking lot of a church. *What kind of a date is this?* Then I saw the Counseling Office sign, and something clicked in my mind. "You're back into your addiction!"

He remained silent. I was furious. "How could you do this to us *again*? This date was even a deception!"

His withdrawal suddenly made sense. He'd broken his first marriage vow he made at our wedding, and now he'd broken his second when he'd promised to be honest. How could I go through his betrayal *again?* Tears seared my eyes as I jerked my hand away from him.

Once again I was seated opposite a counselor.

Once again I was asked if I wanted my husband to leave or to stay.

Once again I was told that I had a scriptural right to end our marriage.

Once again I heard the counselor ask, "What do *you* want?"

What *did* I want? I wanted to scream. I wanted the pain to stop. I wanted him to give his love exclusively to me. I wanted to trust him. I wanted a godly father for our children. I wanted to stop crying so much. What did *I* want? I wanted healing for us.

The words tumbled out, "I want him to stay."

The counselor got right to the point. "Molly, what would you like to say to Timothy?"

"How did this happen?"

"I was doing pretty well, just the usual struggles. But the suicide—it—"

"It started back then? That was four years ago!" I was incredulous.

"I didn't want to tell you because we were so upset already. I even went to a counselor, and she told me not to tell you."

"Do you know what you've put me through this year?"

"I'm so sorry. I completely blew it. I should have talked to you right away. I see that now."

"That's what we promised each other. I'm *so angry.*" The first time he confessed his addiction to me, he didn't know that breaking the silence would help him. This time, however, he *knew* he should be honest but chose not to. "Is there any hope for us? Will you just keep doing this again and again?"

The counselor interrupted, "That's what we do here. We have helped hundreds of sex addicts recover. This pattern can be broken."

"You really can help us?" I asked, turning toward the counselor.

"Yes. Each of you must learn to be whole by finding your identity in God. Only two whole persons coming together can have a healthy relationship."

After I told my story to the group, I was surprised that so much pain could be expressed in minutes. Now it was my turn to look into the faces of the women around me. I saw tears of sorrow, brows furrowed in pain, jaws set in anger, and soft expressions of acceptance. For the first time in my life I was talking to wives of other sex addicts.

I knew they understood as their expressions reflected my feelings. The healing had begun.

chapter 3

FORGIVENESS

"A word of encouragement can heal a wound; a choice to forgive can destroy a stronghold."—John Eldredge[1]

BETRAYAL CONSUMES US WITH HIDEOUS EMOTIONS, and yet the more honest we are, the more we heal. Our feelings are not morally right or wrong. They are legitimate, they are ours, and no one has the right to judge them.

The ugly feelings of repulsion in the beginning are just as valid as the more comfortable ones that will take their place in time. The truth is always appropriate.

I was ashamed to admit how I felt. Was I a failure as a Christian? I poured out my heart to God in my journal and shared with a safe friend who just listened. Often we don't know how we feel until we hear the words come out of our mouths.

Honesty with oneself takes incredible courage. It is the price of a soft heart, unhardened with bitterness. It is the price of the ability to forgive. It is the price of spirituality, and it is the price of the marriage commitment. Some marriages die because a wife can't offer her husband mercy for small grievances while others thrive when a wife forgives the worst offenses.

The actions of others, including our spouses, do not control us. We choose what we do with our feelings. Timothy was repentant and making amends. I didn't know when I'd trust him again, and I was devastated, but, I wanted to forgive him; that was the choice I *wanted* to make.

Integrating Memories with the Truth

Following Timothy's confession, sorrow and loss were my new companions. My former happiness mocked me; it was only ignorance of the truth. The distraction of family responsibilities was a welcome intermission from sadness. However, anger interrupted both grieving and housework; it screamed for my attention.

I went back to the beginning of our marriage and reconstructed memories according to the truth. <u>Honesty, with its painfully high price, was the only way to grieve, rebuild trust, and heal.</u>

I didn't know what to do with the sorrow and loss. I knew God's grace was what I needed, but when I dared to be honest, I felt God had betrayed me too. *Lord, your Word says we reap what we sow. I've never been unfaithful to my husband. How can I trust you when it seems like you've let me down?*

I could connect with God only when I read the psalms where David expressed his anguish. I read Ps. 13:1-3 hundreds of times:

How long, O LORD? Will you forget me forever?
How long will you hide your face from me?
How long must I wrestle with my thoughts
and every day have sorrow in my heart?
Look on me and answer, O LORD my God.
Give light to my eyes, or I will sleep in death.

I often read verses 5 and 6 aloud, hoping to bolster my weak faith:

But I trust in your unfailing love;
my heart rejoices in your salvation.
I will sing to the LORD,
for he has been good to me.

I wanted to forgive Timothy, but my pain argued with my will. Did I have to wait for the pain to subside before I could forgive him? My self-pity was less satisfying with each indulgence. I was miserable. I didn't know what would help. This was one of the worst times of my life. It was hard to believe God cared or that the pain would ever run its course. If I could forgive, would the pain subside?

Understanding the Addiction

Timothy was reading *Out of the Shadows* by Dr. Patrick Carnes, a leading psychologist who specialized in the treatment of sexual addiction. He was so impressed that he registered us for one of Carnes' seminars.

"I hope we won't know anyone here," I said, as we warily entered the hotel.

With a gentle voice Dr. Carnes spoke openly about his own history, which disarmed us. He drew an octopus shape on the board and explained that pain is in the middle. When it gets unbearable, addicts try to comfort themselves but use unhealthy means. For example, sex addicts may view pornography, but if it's unavailable, they may turn to food, alcohol, or work. If one leg of behavior is cut off, another grows proportionately larger. The problem is not the addictive behavior, *the problem is the pain*. The addiction will continue until the pain at its center is dealt with.

The problem is the pain? Sex addiction isn't about sex? It's about pain? I had never heard this before. Timothy wasn't having sex for pleasure—it was a painkiller for him—a drug. I let this new information percolate in my mind. Things that had confused me began to emerge in a different light: We had a good sexual relationship, so the addiction hadn't made sense. But if it was comfort and escape he sought, then it was more understandable. The more he indulged in sexual escapades, the more shame he felt, so the cycle fed itself. Timothy's behavior finally made sense. Alcoholics use alcohol—sexaholics use sex: both trying to escape pain.

Dr. Carnes further explained that children are predisposed to addiction at young ages. If some basic nurturing is lacking, they look outside of themselves for affirmation. If a behavior offers relief from the painful feelings of their shame and unworthiness, then harmful consequences become an acceptable price to pay.

I felt relieved; my fear of rejection was unfounded. I'd been taking his addiction *personally*. My focus shifted from his behavior to its cause; *what agony stirred there?* I've never looked at him the same. He was stuck in a destructive cycle while attempts to medicate his pain made it worse. God knew exactly what I needed to forgive Timothy—I needed to understand his heart.

The truth about sex addiction wasn't as bad as I'd feared. The lies I'd believed were more painful than the truth. My husband's behavior didn't define who I was. Understanding the addiction empowered me, as the truth always does.

Skipping Steps Doesn't Work

David Augsburger has written extensively on forgiveness. He says, "It may sound gracious and loving, but usually the person who forgives prematurely, preemptively, or unconditionally is trying to avoid the hard work of the forgiveness process. It's saying, 'I don't want to struggle.' This leads to a religiously sanctioned form of denial." He continues, "The twelve steps have a much better, and more biblical, instinct about what is appropriate if we have injured someone. The focus is not on asking them for forgiveness but on making amends . . . on demonstrating repentance."[2]

Timothy confessed and is making amends, but that doesn't mean it's easy to forgive him—it means I can stay with him. If he weren't repentant, I would still need to forgive him, but it would violate my boundaries to stay with him.

The Other Women

One night I couldn't get thoughts of Timothy with other women out of my mind. I climbed out of bed and leaned against the doorway. "Lord, please help me forgive Timothy. I want to, but I don't know how."

Immediately I sensed God's answer: "Just accept him."

Is that what I need to do? I turned and looked at my sleeping husband—my recovering sex addict husband—whose behavior had elevated me to life's joyous heights and to bitter depths I didn't know existed. There, in the middle of the night, I chose to accept him; all of him, the good and the hurtful, the whole and the broken parts of him. Peace entered my restless heart. I climbed back into bed next to him and fell asleep.

I tried to accept the sin; God wanted me to accept the sinner.

"Bear with each other and forgive whatever grievances you may have against one another. Forgive as the Lord forgave you" (Col. 3:13). Who can forgive like that? The best I could do was *choose* to forgive him; to *will* to forgive him.

"The command of Jesus is hard, unutterably hard, for those who try to resist it. But for those who willingly submit, the yoke is easy and the burden is light . . . Jesus asks nothing of us without giving us the strength to perform it. His commandment never seeks to destroy life, but to foster, strengthen, and heal it" (Dietrich Bonhoeffer).[3]

When I invited Jesus into my heart as a child, He gave me a new heart. I had taken only small helpings of the grace it held to forgive—until now. His forgiveness is boundless; the only thing that limits it is my will.

"Whatever you did for one of the least of these brothers of mine, you did for me" (Matt. 25:40). The way we treat others is how we treat God himself. The way you treat your spouse is the way you treat Jesus.

Chapter 4

GRIEVING

"She will go in and out of each stage until her heart has
emptied itself of its pain. What she needs most
is a support network."
—Russell Willingham, *Breaking Free*[1]

THE FOUNDATION OF MY MARRIAGE GAVE WAY when
Timothy confessed his unfaithfulness. My thoughts went back to
the beginning of our marriage. I scrutinized my memories in
light of my husband's disclosure. My unwelcome task: to integrate 19 years of marriage with reality.

Recollections surfaced in my mind: Alone in bed at night, I'd
strain to hear Timothy's car turn down our driveway. Frequently
he got home later than he should have. I questioned every late arrival. The details of his infidelity were excruciating, but I had to
know the truth to grieve it and accept it. I devoted time every day
to grieving and feeling my pain. I felt ashamed, embarrassed, and
gullible, but these were the very feelings I needed to face.

I cried a lot, especially at night when the darkness offered little distraction. In the morning I expressed my emotions to God
in the privacy of my journal. The more accurately I defined my
feelings, the easier they were to accept. When they remained un-
defined and unspoken, they were oppressive and stayed with me.

Several times I decided I'd finished grieving, but it was wish-
ful thinking. There were no shortcuts—the feelings simply had
to be *felt*. I couldn't control the process. I had to submit to it
whether I liked it or not, and often I resented it.

Meanwhile, Timothy felt relieved that his secret was in the
light. My sorrow seemed exaggerated compared to his gratitude.
I didn't appreciate that he wasn't as miserable as I was. My sorrow caused a loneliness that became yet another loss to grieve.

24

I'm a Christian; do I really need to grieve? Is my faith just weak? Doubts attacked me while I was practically incapacitated with betrayal.

The Stages of Healthy Grieving

Elizabeth Kubler-Ross identified five stages of the grief process necessary to accept the death of a significant person in our lives. The loss of fidelity in my marriage felt worse than I imagined a death would feel.

I went through each of the five stages of grief: denial, anger, bargaining, depression, and acceptance. Donald M. Joy says in his book *Bonding: Relationships in the Image of God,* "It is my observation that grieving takes a lot of time, and there is a yo-yo effect by which a person who has worked all the way up to acceptance may have a sudden flashback to denial or anger or bargaining. With each descent into the pit, it is necessary to work the way back up."[2]

Denial insulates a person from shock, like an anesthetic. When Timothy disclosed his sexual addiction, my recurring thought was, "I can't believe this is happening." I didn't even cry. I'd been in denial for 19 years: the first year of our marriage he told me he'd "touched a woman's breasts" in the park. I *never* mentioned it again, I hardly *thought* about it again.

The next morning Timothy tried to put his arm around me; I pushed it off. Suddenly *anger* consumed me. I was angry at least six months. Hundreds of times I said, "How could you?"

Timothy relapsed twice, each time for several years. When he finally confessed, the grief process began all over again, except I became increasingly angry and discouraged.

Bargaining is the last of the three steps that are focused on oneself. "God, I'll serve you if he just repents." My propensity for victim thinking made this an unpleasant stage. I thought my nagging threats were appropriate, but when I attended Twelve Step groups I learned I used shaming to try to manipulate my husband and control his addiction.

Depression is the fourth stage: "Depression is essential to recovery from grief. These negative thoughts are the first break-through to the 'world of others.' . . . Depression needs under-standing and affirmation from a few close and trusted friends."[3] I thought I'd never stop crying. I remember saying many times, "I want to go someplace where I can cry all day."

Acceptance allows us to acknowledge that something good came from the relationship. "I wouldn't have identified my shame-based beliefs without the addiction."

Nurturing Myself

I joined a garden club where I could be my new solemn self. I shared this poem at one of our meetings:

What My Garden Has Given Me

When the pain of life was too much to bear,
God looked out my window, "Plant it there.
A lovely garden is what you need,
To plant and nurture and tend and seed,
And when the seeds give birth to leaf,
You'll feel some joy replace your grief,
And when the days seem oh, so long,
Tending your garden will hurry them along.
When your faith grows dim and very weak,
Look at a flower and hear it speak:
'Could you have made one petal of mine?
Why do you try to do the divine?
Place your thoughts in God's hands again,
Trust Him to tend your garden within.'"
Even in the garden I seemed to strive,
For perfection had often been my guide.
I asked Him how the garden should be,
He laughed and smiled down on me,
"My joy doesn't come from instructing you,
But watching with pleasure the things *you* do,
The only reason I made the creation,
Was for your joy and inspiration,

But now it's *your* turn to till the earth
And *My* turn to watch your garden birth."

When I felt utterly bereft, I called my closest friend, and she simply listened to me cry. Sometimes she whispered a prayer or said my name, and I made it through another long day of unquenchable sorrow.

Marsha Means describes the process in *Living with Your Husband's Secret Wars*. "The grief and emotional agony a wife experiences when she discovers her husband's sexual misconduct overwhelms her and leaves her reeling . . . she feels as if her whole world is disintegrating . . . Though grief arrives with a vengeance, it is not our enemy. It offers the only healthy way to work through our loss. Experiencing grief doesn't mean you have no faith; just the opposite is true. God gave us the ability to grieve to help heal our broken hearts."[4]

Triggers

O Lord, I'm dreading it. Anniversaries are
such powerful triggers for me.
"Intimacy with Me is what you can celebrate."

A scent, a song, or a picture reminds me of a time . . . and the memory overwhelms me with sorrow and melancholy. We can't anticipate them, but triggers have a very powerful effect on our emotions. We're suddenly plunged into feelings over which we have no control.

My most dramatic trigger was my sister-in-law's wedding. Six months after Timothy's disclosure, the pastor who married us performed her ceremony. I heard his familiar voice repeat the same traditional vows he said at our wedding 20 years earlier. They'd been violated countless times by my husband. I cried the whole next week.

I was finally comforted when I learned God shared my feelings of grief.

chapter 5

COMFORT

"Afflictions are but the shadows of God's wings."
—George MacDonald[1]

The summer of Timothy's confession I was scheduled to speak at the Communion service for a women's retreat. I was excited to share my new appreciation for the blood of Christ. No matter how repulsive our sin, His blood washes us white as snow.

After the Last Supper, "Jesus went with his disciples to a place called Gethsemane, and he said to them, 'Sit here while I go over there and pray'" (Matt. 26:36).

He desired their *presence.*

"He took Peter and the two sons of Zebedee along with him" (v. 37).

Jesus wanted his best friends nearest to Him.

"My soul is overwhelmed with sorrow to the point of death . . . keep watch with me" (v. 38).

Jesus was God, yet He was full of sorrow? That's how I feel—except I feel guilty—afraid my faith is weak.

"He fell with his face to the ground and prayed, 'My Father, if it is possible, may this cup be taken from me. Yet not as I will, but as you will'" (v. 39).

He *fell?* With His face to the *ground?* I've pictured Jesus kneeling by a rock, His upturned face serene, His hands clasped in prayer, His robe gracefully arrayed around Him. But that's *not* what it says. Prostrate, desperate, with His mouth in the dirt, He pleaded with God. "My Father, if it is not possible for this cup to be taken away unless I drink it, may your will be done" (v. 42). He didn't want the Father's will. He dreaded the pain, rejection, and betrayal.

I do too. I don't want herpes, or any STD. I don't want

thoughts of other women with my husband. I don't want my partner in life to be a sex addict.

Jesus asked God again—and then again! Wasn't there any way other than the Cross? Jesus didn't *want* it; that didn't make Him rebellious, it made Him honest. In spite of His feelings, He surrendered to His Father (vv. 36-42). He obeyed because He *surrendered*, not because His feelings changed.

Dr. Henry Cloud writes, "God wants a relationship with us, and a relationship requires two free people. When Jesus was in the Garden of Gethsemane, He submitted to the will of the Father, but He was acutely aware of His own wishes. 'Let this cup pass' expressed His own desire, which He later surrendered to the Father. He owned and expressed His wishes . . . God wants us to be real people and own what is ours. Only then can we give it away."[2]

By Sunday morning I understood anew the cost of the bread and the cup. They had represented Christ to me, fully God. Now they also represented Jesus—fully man.

Expectant faces looked up, and I began, "Gethsemane means 'oil press.' In the garden, Jesus was already being crushed and bruised for us. Soon the precious oil of the Holy Spirit would be poured out on the Church."

Women wept as they realized Jesus shared their struggle to surrender despite their pain. "He is seated at the right hand of the Father interceding for us right now, and He knows exactly how we feel."

Then we *celebrated* Communion. Jesus' body was broken because He shared our humanity. He demonstrated how to interact with God in our deepest anguish: with honesty, pleading in desperation, expressing *all* that's in our hearts, even our dread of His will. He hears us, He accepts us, and He understands us. Then, even though it doesn't *feel* like it, we can surrender to His will. The joy that follows obedience surprises us. He shared our humanity so we could share His holiness.

My anger toward God was gone. He comforted me in my sorrow and grief by sharing it with me, and in that fellowship I felt understood. I could now accept God's will. I *wanted* to surrender my will to Him.

In his book *Shattered Dreams*, Larry Crabb explains, "We sometimes experience now what seems like hell. But it isn't the hell of judgment; it's the hell of mercy. . . . <u>Shattered dreams subject us to a pain that weakens our stubborn grip on life as we want it and stirs our appetite for the thrill of God's presence.</u> . . . Through the pain of shattered dreams, God is awakening us to the possibility of infinite pleasure." He describes me very well: "In their anguish, people on the spiritual journey abandon themselves to God."[3]

"I am the vine; you are the branches. If a man remains in me and I in him, he will bear much fruit; apart from me you can do nothing" (John 15:5).

Andrew Murray's classic devotional *Abide in Christ* explains that Christians are grafted into Jesus, the Vine. "The more similar the resemblance between the wounded stem and the wounded graft . . . the more complete will be their union."

And just as one might say to a graft . . . as it is fixed in its place, "Abide in the wounds of the stem that is now to bear you;" so to the believing soul the message comes, "Abide in the wounds of Jesus; there is the place of union, and life, and growth . . . The wounded stem and the wounded graft are cut to fit into each other, into each other's likeness. There is a fellowship between Christ's sufferings and your sufferings."[4]

chapter 6

CODEPENDENCE

"Thinking our own thoughts is the beginning of freedom and responsibility."—Dr. Henry Cloud, *Changes That Heal*[1]

HE CAUSED THIS SORROW! He should be making me feel better. Sarah held her husband responsible for her feelings. After all, he *owed* her—big time. She didn't know anyone who would forgive the kind of violations she had. *He doesn't act very remorseful. He should apologize more.*

Sarah went to see her counselor, determined she would find support for her accusations. After she stated her case, Russell said, "I think the Lord wants you to deal with your idolatry."

Sarah swallowed and tried to remain composed. She couldn't believe what she heard. *My idolatry? What about my husband's adultery?*

"You're putting your husband in God's place. You're expecting him to meet all your needs as proof of his love and faithfulness. No one can do that except God."

She sat there stunned. "You mean—are you saying—he isn't responsible for my feelings? He's done horrible things!"

"Yes, he has; sinful and hurtful things. And he is responsible for his behavior. But he is not responsible for your feelings."

Sarah groped to understand Russell's words. She sensed he wanted her to grasp some truth she'd overlooked.

"Has Bill taken responsibility for his behavior?"

"Yeah—but I still feel so rejected." Tears brimmed in Sarah's eyes.

"Of course you do. Your husband was unfaithful to you. Betrayal causes a tremendous loss; one that needs to be painfully grieved. Your feelings are legitimate, but they are *yours*, not Bill's. You are the one who needs to take responsibility for them."

"That doesn't seem fair."

"Is he determined not to act out sexually any more?"

"He says he is."

"That's a substantial part of his repentance. Are you taking that for granted?"

"It seems like the least he can do."

"I counsel many women who would envy your situation. He also goes to a support group where he's accountable. That demonstrates significant repentance."

"I've never thought of it that way. I just expected him to."

"Your expectations are pretty unrealistic. You've assumed he should be responsible for healing *both* of you. He can only change himself."

Sarah let his words sink in while she wiped hot tears from her face. *This feels so unfair.* "I know I can't change him, but I never thought of it the other way around. Are you saying he can't make this pain stop that *he caused?*"

"He can help—to a point. But God is the only one who can meet all of your needs."

That makes sense. I've never been so devastated.

"Intimacy with God is the only thing that completely satisfies us in any situation."

How can I argue with that? Sarah returned his compassionate gaze with red eyes.

"I suggest you apologize for holding Bill responsible for your feelings. Tell him you've put him in God's place and you'll stop demanding from him what only God can provide. Explain you want to stop controlling his recovery, and you're giving the responsibility back to him. You can't change him anyway. And likewise, you're going to take responsibility for your own recovery. And then, Sarah—" she looked at him with a strength of character she didn't even know she possessed, "thank him for the action he's taken so far."

Sarah left Russell's office holding tissues she was sure to need. The drive home gave her time to sort out her thoughts. She was embarrassed that Russell hadn't taken her side; she was used to Bill being the one in the hot seat. However, she felt strangely relieved, *I don't need Bill to feel better.* She didn't have to be trapped in this pain. Her feelings were up to *her*; he didn't have any power to heal her pain, but that was OK, because *she* did! The first smile in a long time slowly spread across her face, revealing a new hope.

The Seeds of Codependence

"Codependence" means "with-dependence." We depend on others at times, but if we usually turn to others to meet our needs, we are not taking responsibility for ourselves—we have given it to others.

We begin our lives totally dependent. We learn trust when our needs are met. As we learn to meet our own needs, we develop self-trust. But if our nurturing falls short, we internalize that something's wrong with us, otherwise our needs would have been met; then our sense of worth suffers. Instead of learning we can trust ourselves, we look to others for our sense of worth. We give them power over us.

Healthy families are not perfect, but they offer grace instead of criticism. Christian parents can introduce children to Christ, who perfectly accepts them. "God alone can heal our shame core with its damaged self-worth. Only His view of us fills the need we have for a parent to affirm and accept us unconditionally. In short, we need to stop looking to others . . . to give us a sense of personal worth, and instead claim God's view of us according to His Word."[2]

Realizing we are cherished by God helps us accept ourselves, and self-acceptance is *not* optional for wholeness. John Powell writes, "This need is a *true and deep love of self, a genuine and joyful self-acceptance, and authentic self-esteem,* which result in *an interior sense of celebration: 'It's* good to be me . . . I am very happy to be me!'"[3]

Sarah remembered their visit to their first counselor. She'd sobbed to Susan, "Is his addiction my fault? Don't I meet his needs?"

"No, Sarah. You don't make Bill's choices for him—he is the only one responsible for his behavior. Bill lacked some essential nurturing when he was a very little boy, long before the two of you even met."

Sarah was relieved. In her support group there were women whose husbands blamed their addictions on their wives. She was beginning to understand that a wife is not responsible for her husband's behavior, *and neither is the husband to blame for the wife's response.* Each of us is responsible for our own feelings and choices.

Susan had said, "Only two *whole* people can make a healthy relationship."

Sarah thought her husband was the only one who was broken. She hadn't understood that Susan was also talking about her. *Now I realize I'm broken too. I knew I was codependent with my friends, but I didn't know I was codependent with my husband.* She blamed Bill for her feelings without question. Her codependent beliefs were a part of her belief system. *That needs to change!*

She'd been obsessed with Bill's sexual addiction, but now she focused on herself. *He's depending on sex to feel better, and I'm depending on him to feel better. We're doing the same thing! Neither of us is letting God meet our needs.*

By the time Sarah arrived home she no longer looked down on Bill. They were equally broken, both in need of healing. If their deepest needs were met in an intimate relationship with God, then neither of them would depend on others or activities that couldn't satisfy them anyway.

She made her way to the patio with a glass of iced tea, opened her journal, and picked up her pen.

Lord, so much has changed since this morning. I thought if I kept trying, Bill would eventually learn to meet my needs. Thank you for this new hope. Please forgive me for putting people and things in your place. I don't have to go without emotionally because of his limitations; you want to meet my needs. Help me tear down my other idols: shopping, decorating, eating . . . I want to have the relationship with you I've longed for—that Jesus gave everything for. In Jesus' name, amen.

chapter 7

THE ADDICTIVE SYSTEM

"You will never know what your husband looks like unless you try to draw him, and you will never understand him unless you try to write his story."
—Brenda Ueland[1]

"One of the most clearly identifiable aspects of shame in families is addictive behavior." —Merle Fossom and Marilyn Mason, *Facing Shame*[2]

I FIRST UNDERSTOOD MY HUSBAND when we attended a seminar by Dr. Patrick Carnes. We'd focused on his sexual behavior; we were shocked it was only a symptom. Healing requires treating the cause: his pain.

His pain? I'm devastated, and I'm supposed to understand his pain? Isn't it my turn for comfort? This feels like another betrayal!

It's an enormous challenge to acknowledge the wounds of your partner in the midst of your own pain. Many choose to remain in the relationship if the sexaholic takes responsibility for his or her behavior by demonstrating repentance: attending recovery groups, counseling, not traveling alone, even arranging lie detector tests to rebuild trust. Meanwhile, you may have to meet the needs of children, work, or both. You need to forgive, grieve, be honest, run a household, and nurture yourself. Can you trust God again? Should you abstain from sexual relations? Should you tell anyone? You've *never* been in so much pain and had so much responsibility.

The common cry: "Is the sex addiction my fault?" Most of us think our partner's recovery is all the relationship needs to heal.

Understanding the addictive system answers many questions, but it's likely to unveil our own dysfunction.

"Sex is the number one reason adult Americans use the Internet, one-third of all visits are to sexually oriented Web sites. . . . Half of cybersex addicts are men, half are women," according to Prodigals International, a Christian resource ministry for sex addiction recovery, who also reports 25 percent of married men have had affairs since becoming Christians.[3]

Sex addicts and coaddicts come from dysfunctional families. More than 90 percent reported emotional abuse, more than 70 percent physical abuse, and 81 percent sexual abuse.[4]

Dysfunctional families have a faulty core belief system of shame that children internalize at young ages. These children develop a distorted sense of reality:

- They aren't worthwhile persons.
- No one would accept them if they really knew them.
- They can't depend on others to meet their needs.
- They believe sex is their most important need.

Impaired thinking deludes the addict to justify his or her inappropriate sexual behavior. As he or she escapes the pain the shame creates, life gets more out-of-control. This unmanageability creates more shame, until the pain is so intense it needs to be relieved with pleasurable behavior. More guilt and shame result, confirming the addict's belief that he or she is a bad, unlovable person, and the addictive system perpetuates itself. "Sex is what makes the isolation bearable."[5]

How can people with good values violate their own standards? They rationalize until they have created a mental compartment where their sexual misconduct is stored. My husband removed his wedding ring as he entered that compartmentalized area of his life. He even used another name: he called himself "Mike" in honor of the first boy who handed him a pornographic magazine. After he acted out, he fled with increased shame back into his ordinary life, replacing his wedding ring as he mentally exited the compartment.

Families with fundamental beliefs suppress "bad" negative

feelings, like anger. The result: gentle, oversensitive men who repress negative feelings. Helping professions like counseling, teaching, and the clergy attract these people, but also place them at risk. Jennifer Schneider writes, "For the budding sex addict . . . the opportunities are plentiful to carry out his compulsive behavior."[6]

The addictive system consists of:
- a faulty core belief system—shameful feelings of low self-worth
- impaired thinking—deludes the addict to continue believing lies that support faulty beliefs
- unmanageability—the result of increased attention to the addiction at the expense of work, relationships, and responsibilities
- the addiction cycle—a self-destructive means of relieving pain

Dr. Carnes explains the addiction cycle has four steps and grows stronger with each repetition. This is the symptom we see—the sexual activity—so it's logical to focus on the behavior instead of the beliefs that caused it. According to Dr. Carnes,[7] the steps of the addiction cycle are:

Preoccupation: an obsessive search for sexual stimulation
Ritualization: routines that add arousal and excitement
Sexual compulsivity: achieving orgasm
Despair: hopelessness about their powerlessness

The addiction cycle is difficult to stop once it begins. Effective change treats the entire addictive system, especially the beliefs that support it.

> "A man is a slave to whatever
> has mastered him" (2 Pet. 2:19).

The beliefs *cause* the behavior; they enslave the addict more than the behavior, which can be substituted if unavailable. Cross-addictions are common with drugs, gambling, alcohol, overeating, and the like.

"Until we deal with these core issues, our attempts at change will probably result in little more than addiction swapping; we manage to give up—say alcoholism—but because we didn't treat the underlying pain, we simply replace alcoholism with another pain deadener such as workaholism."[8]

Our first counselor was a behavioral psychologist. Since he only treated Timothy's behavior, not the shameful beliefs that caused it, he reinforced the strict authoritarian rules imposed by Timothy's dysfunctional parents. It did more harm than good. Predictably, Timothy relapsed, taking years to confess.

When the addict's secret life is exposed *and* he experiences acceptance, he can share his painful feelings. A new cycle is born: self-disclosure allows understanding, resulting in intimacy and self-acceptance.

Steve Arterburn states, "Only when the compulsion is acknowledged, only when recovery is initiated, is there any hope for an authentic love relationship. Then there is hope for self-acceptance, and for sharing who you truly are with another human being."[9]

Patrick Means explains, "By dragging their feelings out into the light rather than leaving them hidden, they found out their feelings lost their power."[10]

There were times I thought I'd never recover from the infidelity. Embracing the pain is the price I paid to become aware of my dysfunction. It is the price for admission into a healthy belief system. It is the price I paid to stop an addictive system poised to enslave my children. It is the price I paid to have a healthy marriage, and it is the price I paid to have intimacy with God and others. It was worth every tear.

Now you can see why understanding the addiction system was the turning point of my relationship with Timothy; it was *the* turning point of my life.

Dysfunctional Family Traits

"We either speak out our feelings or
we will act them out."—John Powell[11]

Understanding the addictive system challenged my "reality," which was based on lies I'd internalized as a child. I thought our families were normal; I was shocked my family was just as dysfunctional as Timothy's.

John Powell says, "Everything depends upon and flows from our openness to ourselves. When we lose the ability to appreciate ourselves and enjoy being ourselves, all sorts of dark and painful things rush in to fill the void."[12]

Faulty core beliefs are the source for addictions and codependence. Dysfunctional families share a characteristic set of these traits:

- Mistaking intensity for intimacy (giving one another permission to live on the edge in order to feel *something*)
- Abandonment
- Drug dependency (includes alcohol and nicotine)
- Authoritarian parenting
- Sex is shameful
- Hypervigilence ("reading" the feelings of others to determine "our own" behavior)
- Unresolved family secrets
- Discounted feelings (feelings shamed; invalidated)
- Gender rejection (Timothy's father was abandoned in an orphanage by his father; he obviously favors girls)
- Control
- Early sexualization (inappropriate nakedness in home to sexual abuse)
- Scapegoat in family (my sister took the brunt of the blame)
- Hypercritical (conditional acceptance; appearance, especially weight, were supremely important)
- Painful, unresolved issues (conflicts rarely resolved)
- Performance over person (unreasonable expectations, work highly valued)

- Neglect
- Over-mothered and under-fathered ("Their mothers, with good intentions, tried to step into the gap left by an absent father . . . The son becomes the mother's confidant and emotional caretaker, and never bonds with his father. These men graduate to manhood not only with a wounded masculinity but also with an unhealthy dependency on women's approval.")[13]

Timothy was extremely close to his mother. When I expressed emotion, he withdrew in anger. I assumed he was uncomfortable with feelings because his family seldom expressed emotion, until I read this: "I had entered adulthood with an unhealthy dependency on women's approval and a reaction of volcanic anger toward women's anger . . . But what was really going on was a little boy's outmoded survival skills."[14] Desperate for approval from mother figures, Timothy panics at any sign of anger. I wonder if his need for women's approval was why he solicited prostitutes. They never turned him down.

In her book *Women, Sex, and Addiction*, Charlotte Kasl says, "Sexually addicted adults are essentially children hiding out in grown-up bodies, hungrily seeking parents to love them unconditionally."[15]

God Protects Us

I have all the dysfunctional ingredients to be addictive. I am fortunate that the Lord made it clear to me early in my Christian walk that I was not to drink alcohol.

There were many years of my life that were laden with losses: Two sons involved with drugs attended recovery groups before I ever dreamed we needed them. Timothy disclosed his sex addiction, my son's friend committed suicide in our home, and we sold our business but lost much of the profit to illegal practices of the buyers. Timothy relapsed into his sexual addiction. We moved into a small house with five children and started over.

If drinking alcohol had been an option for me, I would've escaped a lot of pain—for a time. The cost would have been my family, my health, and my true self.

Several times my mom told me, "What you really need is a glass of wine."

What I really need is to feel this pain and not attempt to escape it.

God knows our weaknesses. We are not doomed to repeat the futile dysfunction we inherited. He rescues us—even from ourselves. I've modeled raging, victim thinking, compulsive eating, and spending—among other defects—to my children, but they have a God who intervenes where I fail. If God impressed on me not to drink alcohol and repeat my family of origins method of numbing pain, then He can protect them from my defects. He wants to set us free to live as He intended: glorious reflections of His love.

chapter 8

COADDICTION

"All of us suffer from addiction . . . the psychological, neurological and spiritual dynamics of full-fledged addiction are actively at work within every human being . . . Moreover, our addictions are our own worst enemies." —Gerald G. May, *Addiction and Grace*[1]

I AM NOT JUST CODEPENDENT; I am as addicted as Timothy. I use things other than sex to medicate my pain, but that's what makes my behavior addictive: I escape from it instead of facing it.

We are all broken, but forever remain the beloved of God. Accepting this as our identity is what heals us. Brennan Manning writes, "The self-acceptance that flows from embracing my core identity as Abba's child enables me to encounter my utter brokenness with uncompromising honesty and complete abandon to the mercy of God. As my friend, Sister Barbara Fiand, said, 'Wholeness is brokenness owned and thereby healed.'"[2]

I thought admitting my brokenness healed me, but time passed and our problems remained. It required three more years of recovery to be honest *with myself*. My feelings were buried; my parents' emotions dominated our family, so I learned to disregard my own. As Patrick Means says, "You can't heal what you don't feel."[3]

The behavior of others defines the worth of codependent persons. Dr. Carnes states, "Co-addicts feel that having a spouse who is sexually out of control is a statement about themselves."[4] If we have a spouse who is a sex addict, something is wrong with us. We try to control them, because we falsely believe our identity is at stake. Control feels shaming to the sexaholic and feeds the addiction cycle. A codependent person who attempts to change the behavior of the addict, but in reality contributes to their addiction, is a coaddict.

"Co-addiction is an obsessive illness in which reaction to addiction causes the loss of self . . . The co-addict is part of the addict's double life."[5] A coaddict's behavior not only encourages his or her addiction, but is what brought the coaddicts together in the first place.

I was content to stop humbling myself at brokenness. At least it's common to us all, whether or not we realize it. When I learned coaddiction develops in dysfunctional families I felt ashamed; I was ashamed—that I had shame. If I needed proof I was dysfunctional, there it was!

My family had problems, but didn't everyone's? I never questioned that we might not be a normal, healthy family. I read the characteristics of shame-based families: no affirmation, performance over person, scapegoat in family, anticonflict rules, no validation of effort, cannot make mistakes, cannot do it right, must always do better, limited expressions of care, conditional support, abandonment, neglect, attacking, hypercritical, unprocessed secrets, extreme standards of performance, emphasis on right or wrong, low "us" concept, constriction of feelings, painful, unresolved issues, needs denied, criticized, and personal limits not respected.[6] Amidst wonderful memories, my family of origin had nearly all of them! *Could that be right?*

I picked up *Silent Shame* by Patrick Carnes and this time I read the list aloud to my husband: negative self-concept, highly performance conscious, unawareness of personal boundaries and own feelings, sacrifice of personal needs, perfectionism, frequent fatigue, addictive behavior, distrust of people, possessiveness in relationships, high need for control. Every single one described me.

"What do you think of that list?"

"I think it sounds like your family."

One memory after another surfaced: the time Dad got a traffic ticket, "Come on, you guys, why didn't you tell me there was a policeman behind us?" *Blame*. I felt ashamed I caused his ticket. He taught me to mix his drinks when I was 12: *guilt* as I enabled his drinking.

Once again, it was my unwelcome task to integrate 20 years of life with reality; this time with my family of origin. *I feel like a traitor. There are thousands of positive things about my family. Can't I just focus on those and forget the shameful ones?* TINA

Then I remembered telling my son that day, "Do you know how much I do for you? The least you can do is—" *Manipulation by guilt. Control. Shame.* Sadness overwhelmed me.

I cried as I remembered childhood events. My dad often said, "If I want something done right, I'll have to do it myself." TINA *Victim thinking. Shame. Distrust of others.* These were just a few of the many dysfunctional beliefs I internalized. Feelings of disloyalty accompanied each memory. I was betraying the family rules: don't feel, don't talk, and don't tell. Keep up appearances.

I cried for two months, grieving my newly realized losses. I was so angry! I went through the stages of grief all over again. And again, I resented that I had to do it at all.

I talked about it with my mother and sister during that time. I don't recommend that. I was angry and blaming, which only hurt our relationships more. The only way to get through the grief process was to feel the sadness of the losses until I accepted them.

The truth is healing; there was dysfunction, but I've also inherited noble traits. Dysfunction is generational, and my parents did break some unhealthy beliefs they were raised with. No family is perfect; we all descended from Adam and Eve. But God's grace is redemptive; He uses even our shortcomings for our good!

As I've accepted the dysfunction in my family of origin, I've quit blaming my parents. Imperfection is just a part of this fallen world, and my children will have losses to grieve about *our* family dynamics.

I forgave my parents, as specifically as I could, with the help of a counselor. Then I asked God to forgive me for the unrealistic expectations and faulty thinking I accepted into my own belief system that had led me to reject myself. I'm finally healing from the codependent mentality that I must be who others want me to be.

This prayer helped me recover my true identity: "Loving God, show me the truth about myself, no matter how beautiful it may be" (Cec Murphey).[7]

"It is tempting for the co-addict . . . to cast all the blame at her straying spouse . . . her choice of partner is no accident. The co-addict's core beliefs do not begin when she marries an addict . . . The seeds of the future co-addict can be found in her family of origin."[8]

Dysfunctional families find reality too painful to confront. They are safe harbors for addictions such as alcoholism, perfectionism, mental or chronic physical illness, emotional abuse, physical abuse, sexual abuse, and extreme religious fundamentalism. Oppressive family rules enforced with parental disapproval prevent expression of feelings or problems. Children learn to sacrifice their feelings, needs, and sometimes their sexuality or physical bodies to make the parents feel good about themselves.

Dysfunctional families produce dysfunctional children who grow up to be dysfunctional adults—unless their shameful core beliefs are replaced with truth. This is our challenge as coaddicts: We don't know we're dysfunctional because we've learned to deny reality. When life becomes so painful we can no longer deny it, God *blesses* us with reality. It didn't feel like sex addiction could be a gift, but it made me aware of my dysfunction. I've only experienced a few years of glorious freedom from shame, but I can already say that a sexaholic spouse was a small price to pay.

Russell Willingham writes, "He is holding onto his addiction in an attempt to meet needs and avoid his loneliness. She maintains her unhealthy hold on him for the same reasons. Both have a deep, God-given need for love and are looking to the wrong sources to meet it. When she really understands this, she sees that she is really no better than her husband; they are both idolaters."[9]

This betrayal is so painful! I deserve some chocolate and a little shopping. Did I even pray? My faulty beliefs told me it's shameful to have needs, so, afraid of God's disapproval, I opted for less risky chocolate. I was vulnerable to self-pity and victim-thinking. I would shop and eat to medicate my pain. My denial resulted in emptiness, overspending, and guilt. To heal my broken heart I needed intimacy with God, but I sought short-term relief in idols. I soon recognized the obvious ones—obsessive gardening, spending, and eating—but controlling? It was difficult to identify the idol of my own strong will.

I found it challenging to raise teenagers. I thought I simply lacked parenting skills until Jane Nelson's books diagnosed my problem: I was controlling and authoritarian. Alarmed, I worked hard to learn democratic skills and communication that respected my children's individuality and boundaries. Relationships dramatically improved—with my kids.

I was clueless I was trying to control my husband. I didn't only parent the way I was parented, I reproduced my family of origin's entire belief system!

"The most startling part of talking to the partners of sex addicts was that co-addicts are mirror images of the addicts themselves . . . that unerringly they find each other."[10] Dr. Carnes continues, "Relationships that are controlling and emotionally unsatisfying create comfort in that they are familiar."

Dr. Carnes writes, "Addicts and co-addicts share three core beliefs . . . But the co-addict develops a different fourth core belief: sex is the most important sign of love . . . When the addict who believes that 'sex is my most important need' meets the co-addict who believes that 'sex is the most important sign of love,' a powerfully destructive situation is in the making."[11] Coaddicts will be extremely wounded by sexual betrayal as they mistakenly believe it is the proof of love.

As the coaddict's identity is threatened, desperate behavior feeds the spouse's addictive cycle: "If she calls him at work, looks through his belongings, smells his clothing, and in other ways puts herself in the place of a controlling mother, the husband may feel like a little boy who has a right to rebel."[12] A common complaint of coaddicts is, "I feel like his mother." They are simply assuming the role of enabler as their dysfunctional mother modeled for them.

The coaddict is likely to keep silent about her feelings, afraid she might drive her spouse away. Fear of rejection is empowered by low self-worth. One learns to fear confrontation and honesty in dysfunctional families. Keeping suspicions secret not only perpetuates the denial of reality but also makes the person feel ashamed.

A coaddict often works in collusion with her addict, attempting to control the addict. Dressing seductively and sexual play can degenerate into behavior she doesn't feel comfortable with. The addict may then use his spouse's participation to rationalize his own addiction.

One year into my marriage, my husband broke down one night, "I've been unfaithful to you. I'm so sorry."

"What happened?"

He sobbed, "In the park this week I was talking to this gal—and then—I don't know why—I touched her breasts."

The only thing I felt was sorrow *for him*. "It's all right. I forgive you." I hugged him, dry-eyed, and never mentioned it or even thought much about it again.

Two years later I came home early from my night shift, and he wasn't home. He arrived at two A.M., shocked that I wasn't at the hospital. "Where have you been?" I demanded.

"I got lonely. I ended up at one of those massage places."

I was sufficiently worried to switch to the day shift, but it never crossed my mind to call a counselor. I don't remember discussing it again.

At first I didn't think I was a coaddict. How could I have enabled his sex addiction? I didn't even know about it.

My parents were alcoholics, so I learned "nothing is wrong" with inappropriate behavior. I acted "normal" and learned to repress my feelings at home. "If there was a high level of tension in a coaddict's family of origin, she is likely to be comfortable with the uncomfortable. . . . Tension is familiar, similar to what was often experienced while growing up in a dysfunctional family."[13]

I thought my family was normal, so I was caught off-guard when my counselor corrected me.

"I came from a good family background—"

"Uh, I don't think so."

"What do you mean?"

"I know too much about your family to agree with you." Reality finally hit me when I looked at a Christmas picture. My toddlers were climbing all over my dad, who was lying on the floor. They thought it was fun until he didn't respond; he'd already passed out from too much spiked eggnog. My mom, sister, and I pretended he was napping—like we always did—but my kids didn't know the family rules yet.

I now understand that I enabled my husband's addiction because I ignored it; it was "normal." Even changing to the day shift was classic coaddictive behavior. I changed my behavior when he should've changed his. I tried to control him. The consequences should've been his, not mine.

I recovered my identity when the truth gradually replaced my faulty beliefs. Several hours a week at my recovery group is a small price to pay for finding *myself!*

I'm often told, "I wouldn't stay with a sex addict." But if we'd divorced, I wouldn't be aware of my core beliefs or my need for recovery. Eventually I would have walked down the aisle for the second time, addict and coaddict, husband and wife. Our families of origin would feel "normal" as they witnessed the blessed event. Our dysfunctional children would feel "normal" with their dysfunctional stepparents.

Dr. Carnes writes, "What you do not work out in one relationship you will have to work out in the next . . . Without help, the probability of ending up in another dysfunctional relationship is almost certain."[14]

If we'd divorced and I hadn't faced my core beliefs, the only thing that would have changed would be the name of my husband.

The Speck

I see the speck in my husband's eye.
To call it a speck feels like a lie.
That speck has cost me severely,
Is it gone? Can he see clearly?

You say there's a log in my own eye.
I need your strength to even try,
To look at my own sin and shame,
And see that we are both the same.

My husband was my stamp of approval.
My image faltered with his removal.
Were we sinners saved by grace?
No! Just two people saving face.

He had his props, but I had mine.
They worked for a while, but not this time.
We'd lived as if appearances mattered,
But our façade was totally shattered.

Nothing we do and nothing we say
Will ever make us feel OK.
Only when we give up trying
Can grace begin satisfying.

I thought I needed my husband to be
My stamp of approval for others to see.
The speck in my husband's eye was removed,
So *my* eyesight could be improved.

chapter 3

RECOVERY

"We must grasp our fundamental brokenness and stop
pretending we are something else."
—Russell Willingham, *Breaking Free*[1]

"He's not ready; it's too early in his recovery."
—Susan Pizante

WENDY FACED HER COUNSELOR, FIGHTING TEARS.
"Why is he so defensive? He hates my feelings! I know he's sorry
about the addiction, but—I feel rejected."

"He can't do it yet, Wendy."

"What do you mean?"

"He's not ready. He's still operating under his shame-based
belief system. That will change with the recovery process; it
takes time to replace his shame with grace and truth. Meanwhile, talking about his addiction still makes him feel ashamed."

"But what should I do with all this pain?" pled Wendy, who
thought she didn't like Susan very much anymore.

"You're not at the mercy of your husband—you're at the mercy of God. Focus on *your* recovery, not his limitations. You'll
quit blaming him for all your pain as you learn what you've
brought into the relationship. Your needs can be met by your
support group, trusted friends, but mostly by God."

Wendy could only nod.

"With recovery, Ben—and you—will become less shame-
based. When you are both whole, the relationship you want will
be possible."

God Invented Recovery

God created Adam and Eve in His image, and they were naked and unashamed. When they sinned, they lost their relationship with God, and shame replaced their glory.

Before Jesus died in our place, He prayed for us, "I pray also for those who will believe in me through their message . . . I have given them the glory that you gave me" (John 17:20, 22). Our faith in Jesus restores our relationship with God and our glory. Not only that, but our shame is removed, "Anyone who trusts in him will never be put to shame" (Rom. 10:11). The work of all Christians is recovering what we lost in the Fall. We were intended to look like this: "Those who look to him are radiant; their faces are never covered with shame" (Ps. 34:5).

"Sadly, most believers do not understand who they really are, who God made them to be." Shannon Ethridge continues in her book *Every Woman's Battle*: "How we see ourselves affects how we live and the decisions we make . . . Once you allow God to correct your beliefs about yourself, those beliefs will begin driving your decisions, your behaviors will follow directly behind, and you will have victory."[2]

I was a modern-day Pharisee on a crusade to earn God's favor and the approval of others. I settled for much less than God offered. I didn't think I was worthy to receive it, but far worse, I didn't think He thought I was worthy. He offered me the glory of Eden, and I timidly picked my salvation out of His overflowing hands. No wonder Jesus said, "Let the little children come to me . . . for the kingdom of heaven belongs to such as these" (Matt. 19:14). A little child would have scooped up everything his or her chubby fists could hold and gone back for more. I was spiritually starved because I felt guilty accepting God's gifts.

Those of us from dysfunctional backgrounds share a common story: we were born into sin like everyone else, but we were also born into dysfunctional homes and internalized a faulty belief system. Conditional acceptance taught us we had to earn our worth; we were never good enough to accept ourselves. We believed Jesus redeemed our souls to spend eternity with Him; we were saved, but not acceptable. We were redeemed, but not restored. Finally, God blessed us with a crisis more painful than our fear of His rejection. For my husband, it was contracting an STD; for me it was discovering my husband is a sex addict. He is restoring me to the intimacy and glory for which I was created and convincing me I am His beloved.

My faulty beliefs continue to tell me I have to perform to maintain this relationship with Him. But I take comfort in Andrew Murray's words: "No, it is simply weakness entrusting itself to a Mighty One to be kept . . . a consenting to let Him do all for us . . . Our part is simply to yield, to trust."[3]

The moment we believe in God's gracious gift of His Son we are saved; we repent and believe by faith. In contrast, recovering from our faulty beliefs is a *process*.

The following stories shared by coaddicts demonstrate the dynamics of recovering from coaddiction.

Jayne's Family Tradition

A group member just finished reading from the recovery book. The last sentence triggered a sad memory for Jayne. "Our family of origin is our pattern for living, even if we hated it."

My mother never had her own bicycle; she used her brother's. It was too tall, and hurt her crotch.

I'd heard that story often, so I was surprised Christmas morning when I got my first bicycle; it was a boy's bike. It was too tall, and it hurt my crotch.

When I saw my best friend's bike—pink with purple streamers—my suspicions were confirmed: something was wrong with me.

That's not all; my sister got a girl's bike. My mom accused her parents of favoring her brother, but she did the same thing to me.

Jayne saw compassion in the faces of the group. One member was thinking about the time her mother told her she couldn't have a bike because she didn't want to worry about her. She'd internalized it as one more proof of her worthlessness. The truth now brought her one step closer to freedom from shame.

When we relate our stories, we see ourselves through the

eyes of the other group members. We realize the behavior of others defined *them*, not us. The memory is restored according to the truth and loses its power to shame us. The more stories we share, the more lies are corrected. In time, our shameful core belief system is replaced, and freedom from shame allows us to be who God intended.

Amy's Abuse

One group member read a paragraph about shame from abuse. Anyone could comment. Words erupted from Amy; her story begged to be told.

"Sometimes my dad was patient but—" Amy's jaws clenched. "To teach my little sister not to soil her panties anymore, he took them and shoved the feces up her nose. I watched in horror. When he walked out of the room he said, 'All you need to raise kids is a puppy training manual.'

"I was scared of him after that. I tried to protect my sister, but I didn't know what to do when he yelled at us, 'Are you dumb, stupid, or both?'

"The reading said abuse can be a form of control. I think he needed us to be perfect. It's been more than 40 years, and I just realized he abused us; he controlled us by shaming us."

Amy's features hardened in defiance, "I'm still letting him control me—because I feel guilty talking about this!" She burst into sobs.

The other group members let her grieve. They'd learned to feel their pain instead of deny it. Her courage to face the truth about her dysfunctional family was her first step in healing her shame.

God's Patience with Lynette

"I was reducing the clutter in my house and discovered I had 25 antique watering cans! Do you know how much pain I was in to keep buying those things? It was the year I found out Eddy is a sex addict.

"I was embarrassed until I remembered this quote by George MacDonald, 'God lets men have their playthings, like the children they are, that they may learn to distinguish them from true possessions.'[4]

"They served their purpose, but I don't need them anymore; I've finally learned God loves me—even if He doesn't want me to buy something. His presence in my life replaced my watering cans!"

Victoria: Controlled

"I was going into sixth grade and my dad took me shopping for school shoes. I found the ones I wanted, but he kept looking around. 'Dad, these are the ones I want.'

"My heart sank as he picked out a pair of sturdy leather saddle shoes. He placed them on the counter and reached for his wallet.

"Fifteen minutes at the shoe store reinforced my feeling of worthlessness for years.

"Now I let my children pick out any shoes they want."

Juanita's Self-Image

"I always thought I was fat. My dad often told me, 'Hot weather's hard on little fat girls, isn't it, Juanita?' I knew he needed me to laugh—but inside I cried. My mother never said anything.

"Now I know he was trying to control me with shame; it was a threat *not* to get fat. I carried a heavy burden of proof— of his worth.

"I still struggle to believe I'm acceptable. I should have grace for overweight people, but I don't. I learned it was shameful; I have to consciously tell myself: A person's worth cannot be measured on a scale."

The victim becomes the victimizer; the oppressed becomes the oppressor. Your behavior won't change until your belief system does. The renowned Dr. William Glasser says, "People act, and especially relate to other people, in accordance with the way they think and feel about themselves."[5]

My favorite book as a child was *The Boxcar Children*.[6] Thinking they are now orphans, the children flee, finding shelter in a boxcar. They set up house with all sorts of treasures they find in a dump.

As a child, I loved going to the dump with my dad. While he unloaded the pick-up, I scrounged for treasures. Several years ago I made a trip to the dump to help my mom. I wondered what I'd find. Sure enough, I bent down and eagerly picked up some vintage pottery. How fun! As I drove down the hill, I felt like the Lord was speaking to my heart, "I have treasures untold for you, but you are content to pick up potsherds, thinking they are my riches."

I wiped tears from my eyes and considered His words. *O Lord, You're right! And I hold them close as if my life depends on them. Please teach me to recognize your treasures.*

Now you know why I'm so thankful for recovery. I used to collect "potsherds" to escape the pain of my shame and low self-worth. Now I'm learning to accept myself and believe He who is the giver of all things counts me worthy to share intimate fellowship with Him.

chapter 10

RECOVERY HAPPENS IN GROUPS

"Possibly the most significant resource addicts and their
families have in their recovery: their peers."
—Dr. Patrick Carnes[1]

"If the idea of going to a recovery group makes you feel
ashamed, then by all means, go. Your basic core belief is
shame, and recovery will transform your life."
—S-Anon member

OVER THE PAST 15 YEARS, WE'VE WORKED with a number of professional counselors, therapists, doctors, and pastors in an effort to rein in Timothy's addiction and my coaddiction. After his last relapse, he called Roger.

"When have you been able to maintain your sobriety, Timothy?"

"Well—the first four years."

"What kind of recovery work did you do?"

"I went to SAA (Sex Addicts Anonymous) and SLAA (Sex and Love Addicts Anonymous) meetings every week."

"Is that the *only* time you've been sexually sober?"

"Yes. I did have one year of sobriety at a counseling center's group."

"Then Twelve Step groups work for you when nothing else has. I'd like to see you go to 30 meetings in the next 30 days. That'll turn your thinking around."

"I'm so glad I called you. Thank you, Roger."

Timothy wasn't neglecting his recovery; he was attending

support group meetings at church or a counseling center the whole time—and lying. What was wrong? He didn't feel safe enough to be honest. If there is cross-talk, confrontation, advice, offering solutions, or even well-intentioned reading of a scripture, we can feel judged instead of unconditionally accepted. Shame results—the very thing the meeting is meant to heal.

That is why the Twelve Steps works. Anne started S-Anon in my city. She explained why it is imperative to observe the rules of the meetings, "If we don't respect the structure of the S-Anon principles, then we'll simply repeat the same behavior we learned in our dysfunctional families." This was the problem in the meetings Timothy went to, and he didn't feel safe enough to be honest.

It had been years since Timothy attended Twelve Step fellowships, and he'd forgotten how helpful they were. Everyone takes turns facilitating the meeting, so there is no leader. The program is self-governed, so no one has authority. Only donations are accepted. It is self-motivated; each member takes responsibility for his or her own recovery.

Timothy told me about S-Anon, a group for the friends and family of sex addicts. He suggested I go. "A popular image is of the deluded sex addict being confronted by his or her distraught partner and thus coerced into getting help. Yet, often the reverse is true. Addicts will get help but then meet resistance when they ask spouses or partners to get help for themselves—despite overwhelming evidence of need."[2] I confess this was my attitude at first. *Why do I need recovery if he's the sex addict?* I resented the meetings until I broke through my denial.

> **"Addicts and co-addicts find what their obsession could never satisfy: a deep and personal sense of self-worth and value."—Dr. Patrick Carnes[3]**

The Twelve Steps of S-Anon

 1. We admitted we were powerless over sexual addiction—that our lives had become unmanageable.

2. We came to believe that a power greater than ourselves could restore us to sanity.

3. We made a decision to turn our wills and our lives over to the care of God as we understood Him.

4. We made a searching and fearless moral inventory of ourselves.

5. We admitted to God, to ourselves, and to another human being the exact nature of our wrongs.

6. We were entirely ready to have God remove all these defects of character.

7. We humbly asked Him to remove all our shortcomings.

8. We made a list of all persons we had harmed and became willing to make amends to them all.

9. We made direct amends to such people wherever possible, except when to do so would injure them or others.

10. We continued to take personal inventory, and when we were wrong promptly admitted it.

11. We sought through prayer and meditation to improve our conscious contact with God as we understood Him, praying only for the knowledge of His will for us and the power to carry that out.

12. Having had a spiritual awakening as a result of these steps, we tried to carry this message to others and to practice these principles in all our situations.

Copyright by S-Anon International Family Groups, P.O. Box 111242, Nashville, TN 37222-1242, (615)833-3152; reprinted with permission.

"I unabashedly love Twelve Step programs."
—Melody Beattie, *Codependent No More*[4]

The Twelve Steps have helped members for more than 60 years since it was started by Bill W. "It parallels the life-giving dynamics of a healthy family and culture," writes Dr. Patrick Carnes.[5] This is essential to reparenting ourselves in healthy ways.

Dr. Henry Cloud says, "Many Christians do not turn away from the 'tradition of their elders.' They live according to a false religion, the spiritual system of their families. In order to grow, they must renounce the theology of their dysfunctional families and adopt the spiritual principles of God's family."[6] He continues, "Jesus taught we have been transferred from one kingdom to another (Col. 1:13-14). A crowd was gathered around Jesus, and someone told Him that His mother and brothers were outside. 'Who are my mother and my brothers?' He asked. 'Here are my mother and my brothers! Whoever does God's will is my brother and sister and mother' (Mark 3:31-35). A vital part of this transfer is to realize who our 'family' is to be. In a real sense, God is saying that we have to get our family support from the ones who do His will. We have to renounce the rules of relationship we learned in the first spiritual system and learn God's ways of connection."

The Twelve Steps is a process that facilitates development of new, healthy beliefs. Sexual sobriety is a *result* of a healthy belief system—not the *goal.* That's why the Twelve Steps of Alcoholics Anonymous (AA) could be applied to other addictions; it heals our faulty beliefs about our worthlessness, and our shame is replaced by our realization of who we are in God's eyes. Recovery eliminates our *need* to medicate—regardless of the "drug" we use.

Recovery starts as soon as we enter the room and see understanding and acceptance on other faces. It may be the first time in our lives we can be honest *and* completely accepted. As recovery progresses, addicts and coaddicts learn that, "What they really wanted could be found in the support of others. They start to live new lives with focuses on healthy human relationships as opposed to sex."[7]

Coaddicts need to recover *themselves*; to learn who they are independent of their relationships. This process is called *differentiation.* "Always, recovery requires taking care of yourself. And it starts with the basics."[8]

Once Timothy and I are independent, boundaries will maintain our individuality. This is our present stage of recovery, and it is a struggle for two reasons: Coaddicts progress faster than addicts, so often we don't relate to each other. Second, Timothy restarted his recovery for the third time last year, so what stage is he in, anyway? It probably doesn't matter; I need to focus on my own recovery.

We recently attended the very first Recovering Couples Anonymous (RCA) meeting in our area. Sitting there with seven other couples made me realize again, *we're not alone*. And neither are you.

chapter 11

MERCY TRIUMPHS OVER JUDGMENT

> "When your husband is a sexaholic, it's easy to be a
> Pharisee."—Cherry P.

> "Be on your guard against the yeast of the Pharisees,
> which is hypocrisy" (Luke 12:1).

I DON'T FEAR JUDGMENT FROM PEOPLE outside the church; I expect it. I fear rejection from Christians. I'll never forget when Timothy disclosed his sexual indiscretions to me. The sad ordeal began with a phone call from Pastor Sam. The minute I heard his voice I knew something was wrong. "Molly, could you come to my office?"

When unthinkable words fell from Timothy's lips, I knew my life would never be the same. He was so broken my heart ached for him. Even when the devastation hit me, I believed God would help us through the nightmare.

Our pastor's reaction was far different: "You need to resign from the church board." He added, "Don't tell anyone about this. Come back to me for your counseling." The deep sorrow I felt for Timothy suddenly turned to fear—and shame.

We returned to his office the next morning. "I had to tell my wife about you guys."

"What?"

"I told Lynn."

"Why did you—?"

"I needed her support to cope with such serious sin."

There it was again—*fear*.

Safe inside our car, we debriefed, "He told Lynn! I can't believe he did that!"

"I know. I'm so embarrassed."

"Didn't you feel awful when he said, 'such serious sin'?"

"Yeah."

That evening at church we saw Lynn. She didn't say anything to me; I stood there, waiting for the comfort I desperately needed. She only gave Timothy a hug. "We love you, Timothy." But her long glance said, "I know your secret."

You know because Pastor Sam broke our confidence! I felt horrible—betrayed, judged, and ignored. I sat through church trying to hear something to calm my churning emotions—from a pastor I now disrespected.

Before our next counseling appointment, Pastor Sam met with our closest friends, even though he'd counseled *us* not to tell anyone. This was the second time he betrayed our confidence.

"We discussed how we could help you guys," he rationalized.

We left his office in disbelief.

Timothy said, "He met with our friends, *without* asking or inviting us!"

"He went completely behind our backs."

Our pastor's actions shattered our trust in him. Timothy expected his unfaithfulness would devastate me, but our pastor's breach of confidentiality made both of us feel betrayed.

We found another church where we received acceptance from Roger, our new pastor. We were offered confidential support groups; mercy was incredibly healing to my broken heart.

I interviewed counselors on the phone to find one who could help us. During these conversations I heard the term "sex addiction" for the first time. "Yes, sex can be addicting, just like alcohol and drugs," one counselor said. *Maybe that's what's wrong with Timothy.*

The sex addiction consumed my thoughts. Unaware of the depths of my own sinful nature, it would be 14 years before I realized *I* was broken too.

Well-meaning parents taught me with shame;
They likely had their folks to blame.

When I excelled I found approval;
I thought success caused shame's removal.

I learned to be better than everyone else,
To please the tyrant within myself.

Acceptance came at the high price,
Of pride for what I did in life.

I got saved, just in case;
Compared to others I needed less grace.

Then I learned of my husband's addiction,
I even had pity on his affliction.

But I made sure everyone knew,
That I was the stronger of the two.

A decade passed, lonely and weary,
But willing to see myself more clearly.

I thought I'd forgiven my husband, but like a wounded victim, I used his addiction as ammunition to hurt him back. It worked—at the expense of our relationship.

Expressing *legitimate* feelings is constructive, but I indulged in self-pity, blame, and shaming. I took advantage of Timothy's vulnerability—like our pastor did—like the Pharisees did.

I finally wrote in my journal: "Lord, am *I* responsible for something damaging our relationship?"

The word "pride" came to mind.

I think I'm better than him, don't I?

Suddenly things made sense. My pride was so out of control I was even proud I'd forgiven him—that I was so spiritual! When I repented I realized this is where my husband had been—contrite before a holy yet merciful God—while I judged him from a position of superiority.

I handed Timothy my journal. When he finished reading my confession, our eyes met. I whispered hoarsely, "I am so sorry. Please forgive me."

He pulled me to him, showing me the mercy I'd selfishly withheld from him. We finally had the potential for the intimacy my heart longed for—not because he changed—but because I did.

As spouses of sexaholics, we are vulnerable to this pharisaic mentality; the addict's socially unacceptable sin makes us feel respectable by comparison. The betrayal may make us feel we're right and they're wrong—about everything. I thought, "He's blessed to have me." This lie delivers a destructive weapon: pride. I suspect my pride was just as destructive to our relationship as Timothy's addiction.

Brennan Manning writes, "The number of people who have fled the church because it is too patient or compassionate is negligible; the number who have fled because they find it too unforgiving is tragic."[1]

Our present struggle is not new to the Church. "Judgment without mercy will be shown to anyone who has not been merciful. Mercy triumphs over judgment!" (James 2:13).

Some churches even question the validity of Twelve Step programs, a powerful tool for addiction recovery. The unconditional acceptance and confidentiality found in these fellowships enhance emotional safety, so honesty thrives—something many can't find in their churches. They result in a spiritual awareness and dependency on God because they offer mercy, not judgment.

Dr. Henry Cloud writes, "Guilt and shame too often send us into hiding . . . Sometimes the church reinforces our inclination to hide . . . It is interesting to compare a legalistic church with a good AA group. In this kind of church it is culturally unacceptable to have problems; that is called being sinful. In the AA group it is culturally unacceptable to be perfect; that is called denial. In the former setting people look better but get worse, and in the latter they look worse but get better."[2]

I understand now what the apostle Paul meant when he said, "Therefore I will boast all the more gladly about my weaknesses." (2 Cor. 12:9). If not for the addiction, I would still be judging others without mercy. For years, I thought calling him to repentance "helped" him, until I learned it was also a disease.

Marnie Feree writes, "'Is sexual addiction a sin, or is it a disease?' The answer is yes. It is both . . . putting a spiritual Band-Aid on this problem . . . is going to be harmful, because it will contribute to the hopelessness that people feel . . . Sexual addiction is a multifaceted disease, and so it requires a multifaceted solution. There is a physiological aspect . . . a neurochemical component . . . closely related to the changes that take place in your brain when you take crack cocaine . . . There is also an emotional . . . a mental . . . a relationship . . . and a spiritual component. All . . . need to be addressed if the addicted person is to experience healing."[3]

What makes us legalistic? As young adults we tend to replace our parents with other authority figures, especially when we leave home. As Christians we often use the church to reparent ourselves. Those of us who grew up in a rigid, authoritarian home will feel secure in a legalistic church. As we mature spiritually, we internalize more grace and eventually outgrow the external authoritarian parameters we needed in legalism.

Illusive parental approval led me to an extremely fundamental church. It wasn't legalistic enough to suit my needs, so I broke off with a small group. I thought I'd finally found my sense of worth in my superspirituality. I was sincere, I was devout, and I was dysfunctional. The tyrannical taskmaster within me was pious—and proud.

I was a baby Pharisee—learning to wield power for the first time in my life. It felt great to finally have as much authority as my parents, who taught me appearances were more important than honesty. Many relationships were strained or sacrificed before I realized my legalism was only covering up my brokenness with pharisaical whitewash.

Meanwhile my life was based on fear and earning approval—as it had *always* been. For example, one day I earnestly prayed, "Lord, what kind of cookies do you want me to make?" *I bet He wants me to make chocolate drop cookies, and I don't even like them.* I checked the cupboard and to my relief I didn't have any cocoa; "Lord, I really want to know which cookies *you* want me to make."

His words pierced my heart, "You can make any kind of cookies you want to make—*my love.*" I tearfully baked *my* very favorite cookies. My first taste of *freedom from fear*—revealed my spiritual anorexia; I was starving myself of God's love and mercy. In keeping with the pharisaical tradition I'd inherited from my forefathers, I demanded the same sacrifice from others as proof of their devotion to God—and earn my approval.

Thirty years later I'm still learning to accept grace. It's challenging because I rarely saw it modeled. I've long desired to give my children, my friends, my husband, and *myself* the unconditional acceptance I've barely tasted. It's what we need most—and it's my greatest weakness.

<u>Addicts are starved for acceptance.</u> <u>They have already rejected themselves; they are full of shame simply for who they are.</u> More judgment only feeds the addiction. They need the *truth:* God has grace for all sinners, because Jesus paid our debt. Truth without grace results in legalism and shame. Emphasizing grace leads to license, or permission to sin. I needed to balance truth with grace. I spent the first 20 years of my life being judged. The next 30 years I perfected judging myself and others. I'm convinced God doesn't want me to waste any more time punishing myself when I can spend it enjoying Him and loving others.

> "What does God expect from us? Failure!"
> —Russell Willingham[4]

How did Jesus treat people in sexual sin? When the Pharisees brought in a woman caught in adultery, they made her stand before the group and reminded Jesus the Law of Moses commanded her to be stoned.

Jesus replied, "If any one of you is without sin, let him be the first to throw a stone at her" (John 8:7). When only Jesus was left, He said, 'Woman, where are they? Has no one condemned you?'

"'No one, sir,' she said.

"'Then neither do I condemn you,' Jesus declared. 'Go now and leave your life of sin'" (vv. 10-11).

Jesus' grace isn't at the expense of truth. God's mercy doesn't enable sin—it encourages repentance.

David Peck, founder of the Aesthetic View Institute, would say that Jesus didn't "awfulize" her sin.[5] He shows mercy that makes it easier for her to take responsibility for her behavior. When we humiliate others, we "awfulize" their sin. Shaming discourages honesty because it threatens emotional safety. When we awfulize another's sin we feel superior—our pride takes advantage of another's weakness. Jesus didn't allow her accusers to do this. He leveled the playing field; He made it safe to be honest.

Jesus loved the woman caught in adultery *in spite of* her sin. She may experience consequences of her choices, but the withdrawal of God's love won't ever be one of them. God doesn't limit His grace—we do.

Jesus approaches another woman caught up in immorality at a well in Samaria (4:5-42). He broke the social rules and spoke to a Samaritan, a woman no less! If she still doubted His acceptance, her doubt likely vanished when He asked for a drink, rendering Him unclean when He touched her drinking vessel. She felt safe and accepted; she could answer truthfully when Jesus asked about her husband.

I asked David Peck, "How do I help my husband face reality?"

"By not awfulizing it," he replied without hesitation.

Henri Nouwen writes, "Our ministry of reconciliation most often takes place when we ourselves are least aware of it. Our simple, nonjudgmental presence does it."[6]

Jesus told a parable about me in Matt. 18:21-35. I owed Him a debt that was impossible for me to pay—and He forgave it. His mercy is intended to encourage me to forgive a small debt owed me by my husband.

chapter 12

STDS AND HIV
(SEXUALLY TRANSMITTED DISEASES AND HUMAN IMMUNODEFICIENCY VIRUS)

"I'M MRS. MILLER, AND I'M A NURSE. Thank you for inviting me to your class." Thirty eager faces were turned toward me, but the middle school classroom is tense—sex is the topic.

"Please take out a piece of paper." Desks clatter open, "Draw a time line of your life; birth, graduation, marriage, and so on."

I smile and make eye contact before I begin telling them about David and Celeste, who were high school sweethearts. He was on the soccer team, and she loved art and music. After graduation they went to different colleges and dated others. After college they reunited and got married. They wanted to start a family right away.

Celeste went to her first obstetrician appointment with excitement. She was surprised her doctor called the next week, "Could your husband bring you to the office?"

"I'm sorry to tell you this. Your blood work shows you are HIV positive."

"But how can that be?" cried Celeste "Isn't that sexually transmitted? How could I possibly—can I get David?"

David took the chair next to Celeste and the doctor resumed his unpleasant duty. "Have either of you ever received a blood transfusion?"

"Not me!" snapped Celeste while David shook his head.

"What about IV drug use?"

"No."

"We need both of you to get tested to be sure—"

"But this isn't possible!" interrupted Celeste. "Tell him!" She turned desperate eyes to David, but her gaze went unnoticed. David cradled his head in his hands.

The doctor stood up, "Here are your lab slips. Make an appointment in one week."

When the elevator doors closed, Celeste demanded, "David, what have you done?" She instinctively placed her hand on her tummy where their child's life was at risk.

"I had sex with a couple of girls I dated in college. I had no idea—"

"You *what?*"

"I'm so sorry. I had no idea I might have gotten something. I should have—I can see that now."

"We probably have HIV! I can't believe this!"

Like many states, an HIV test was not required for their marriage license.

Seven months later their little girl was born. Celeste received antiretroviral drugs intravenously before and during the birth. Hopefully, any of her blood that contaminated the baby would have a low viral count. As an added precaution the baby received the same medication. Celeste held her tiny daughter and grieved that she couldn't breastfeed her own baby. She promised herself, "Every day together will be a precious gift." With treatment, Celeste hoped to see her daughter's 16th birthday.

HIV Prevention

"Imagine you get infected with HIV the same age David and Celeste were. Draw a cross 10 to 15 years later on your time lines."

Wide eyes look up, but no one speaks.

I break the silence, "How many of you were unaware you infected your spouse with HIV?"

Half the hands went up in answer to the unthinkable question. "This doesn't have to happen to you. HIV can be prevented. Did you know that today most people become infected with HIV by heterosexual transmission—sex between a man and a woman?"

A discussion follows about condoms; they are not safe sex but only *safer* sex. "Abstinence from sexual activity is the only safe behavior there is."

"There are other STDs that condoms don't protect you from at all." This leads into the topic of other STDs. "The ominous thing is the *absence* of symptoms in so many of them, including HIV. The *only* way to know if you have them is to get tested."

I held up a poster from the Centers for Disease Control (CDC). I asked a student to read the inscription under the glamorous woman: "She has all the symptoms of HIV."

"She not only has all the symptoms of HIV but also has all the symptoms of a number of STDs. Many are asymptomatic—that is, they may not have noticeable symptoms."

I repeat the most important question of my presentation, "What's the only way to know if you have an STD?"

"Get tested."

Today, three months is generally accepted as the window of time for our body to make HIV antibodies, which is how the presence of the HIV virus is tested. In rare cases it may take longer. This is not a well-known fact, and it explains why the CDC urges getting tested only where it is accompanied by counseling, like the county health department. An HIV test a few days or weeks after contracting the virus could easily be negative; meanwhile the virus is replicating through the use of the host's own genes, but antibodies are not being made against it—yet. To be accurate, an HIV test must be repeated three months after sexual contact.

"So, how many of you think you would know if you had an STD?"

Not a single hand went up.

"Congratulations! You have knowledge that can let you *live* your time line."

I passed out literature from the American Social Health Association[1] (ASHA). They distribute educational material for the CDC. Here is a summary of the information: Sexual abstinence is the *only* sure way of protection against STDs and HIV. Only a few birth control methods provide *some* protection; the male latex condom and the female condom are rated "very effective" and the diaphragm and cervical cap are rated "fair." All others provide "no" protection from STDs, and they are: spermicides, birth control pills, injectables, hormonal implants, and the IUD.

"Now consider 3 to 14 percent of women become pregnant with male condoms. Since viruses and bacteria are even smaller than sperm, what does that do to the percentage rate for STDs?"

A student offers, "There's more chance of STDs than pregnancy."

"Knowledge is power. Today you've been equipped with the truth about HIV and STDs so that you can make responsible decisions. It takes courage and commitment. I know it's not easy—my husband and I dated for six years before we got married. With God's help you can remain a virgin until your wedding day. If you've already had sex, you can make a new commitment to abstain until you are married. This is called secondary virginity; it's a growing movement that demonstrates great maturity and self-respect."

I answered their questions before leaving.

I often used our marriage as an example. I've never felt more deceived than when my husband confessed his sexual addiction.

I was scared about the possibility of STDs. "Tell me about the tests you got."

"I went to the health department and told them to test me for everything."

"Did they test you for HIV?" I am terrified of the virus that causes AIDS. I never dreamed HIV could be a threat to my life.

"They test it anonymously. They gave me a number and I have to go back to find out the results. They won't tell you over the phone like they do with the other tests." Our eyes met; we didn't need to voice our fears.

"When do you go back?"

"Two more weeks."

How could I wait that long to find out if we were going to die from AIDS?

"You know, they test the antibodies you make against the virus, not the presence of the virus itself. The average person takes 25 days to make antibodies, but some people take three months. In rare cases it might take up to six months." I'd given this well-rehearsed speech many times in public, never dreaming I'd give it to my husband.

"I know. Don't worry; I'll get tested again in three months."

Don't worry?

"We should abstain from sex until then."

"I think so too. A book on sex addiction I'm reading recommends a period of sexual abstinence. It says it's helpful to communicate intimacy in nonsexual ways."

How convenient! "You've been reading a book?"

Timothy's first HIV test came back negative, but I made no assumptions. When it was still negative at three months I felt relieved. At six months he got his last test, and we resumed sexual relations. I was still afraid to have sex with my husband—it seemed like having sex with a time bomb. Even though one in four people have genital herpes in the U.S., I didn't want to be one of them. Because of the herpes, Timothy was free of his shameful secret, which broke the power of it, but it had come with a price.

Many spouses have paid the price for their partner's sexual addiction. In my support group Cathy discovered her husband's addiction when she contracted genital herpes. "It was the worst day of my life. I sat in the kitchen crying in pain from the herpes, looking up divorce attorneys in the phone book."

"He's in counseling but won't go to SA (Sexaholics Anonymous). Cathy remains hopeful, but she knows without recovery he won't be able to maintain his sexual sobriety.

Genital Warts or Human Papilloma Virus (HPV)

I immediately recognized Shannon's voice on the phone, "Molly, I have a medical question for you. I think I have genital warts. How did I get them?" My heart sank.

"The only way they are spread is sexually." I waited for my words to sink in.

"So I got them from my husband?" She innocently asked, "How'd he get them?"

"Well, they're spread by having sex with someone who has them, so—"

"Are you telling me he's having—an affair?"

"Well, he got them from someone, and it doesn't sound like it was from you."

"But we've been married 23 years!"

"I know. Something's wrong."

"I can't believe this."

"I'm so sorry."

"What am I going to do?"

"You have to take responsibility for your health. Warts can have serious consequences."

"Oh, no!"

"They're treatable—they're not curable, but they are treatable."

"OK. So I go see my doctor."

"And what do you want to do about your husband?"

"I know I need to talk to him—but—I just can't believe it."

I was heartsick. I prayed with her before hanging up. Her husband refused to go to counseling and wanted out of the marriage. The divorce was especially painful for their two teenage boys, who felt abandoned by their father. They got counseling and worked through their anger. She got a job, bought a house, and raised two godly young men. Her husband was not faithful to her, but God was.

Some types of genital warts (HPV) increase the chance of cervical cancer, so Shannon was conscientious about getting her Pap smear every year. They provide early detection of precancerous cells, which provides the most effective cure.

Denial of Risk Factors in Society

We live in a sexually charged society. Advertisers use sex to market their products. Movies and television programs frequently contain sexual innuendo or even explicit sex, and *rarely are there any consequences*. These distortions of reality give us permission to deny the risk factors of sex with multiple partners *or one partner who is having sex with others*. This modeling has tragic consequences. Acceptance of casual sex has become part of our subconscious.

"What Happens in Vegas Stays in Vegas" currently publicizes Las Vegas, Nevada. In the only state where prostitution is legal, could there be a more obvious lie? Sexual activities may be kept secret, but not the STDs contracted in Vegas. They go home with their host—incubating quietly—until their symptoms eventually betray their presence—and Vegas's motto. Because many STDs are asymptomatic, they may be transmitted to others before they are finally discovered.

The purpose of this chapter is to make spouses of sex addicts aware of their risk factors. It is not intended to provide information about specific STDs, which continue to increase. The most common are genital warts (HPV), which can be hard to see, chlamydia, a major cause of infertility, and trichomoniasis.

Detection is the major problem with STDs. Even though symptoms may not be noticeable, they can cause internal damage. Common STDs that can be cured are chlamydia, trichomoniasis, gonorrhea, and syphilis. Common STDs that cannot be cured but can be treated are genital warts (HPV), genital herpes, hepatitis B, and HIV.[1]

Sex addiction is a progressive disease. The law of diminishing returns makes the addict increase the stimuli to get the same high. It's common for an addict to confess his less offensive behavior, and then divulge more depending on the reaction he receives. He has grown accustomed to lying, so emotional safety will encourage honesty.

Because of the serious consequences of STDs, it is my opinion that all sexual activity should stop until testing is finished, including a second HIV test at least three months after the last sexual encounter. Testing for STDs is an appropriate way for the addict to make amends and prove the sincerity of his repentance. Even if STDs were not a threat, sexual abstinence has proven beneficial for healing the relationship and is frequently encouraged by counselors.

"Abstinence makes this statement: *If you don't value me and our relationship enough to deal with this issue, I choose not to entrust myself to you sexually.* He can accuse her of controlling and manipulating if he wants to, but the fact is, his choices have forced her to make choices of her own."[2]

To learn more about STDs, call:
CDC National STD and AIDS Hotlines
1-800-227-8922 or 1-800-342-2437

The American Social Health Association
(ASHA) 1-800-783-9877
www.ashastd.org

chapter 13

SEXUAL HEALING

> "There are no emotional condoms that can make sex emotionally safe . . . To make sex emotionally safe you have to make a relationship emotionally safe. And that involves a lot of hard work."
> —Dale Ryan, Christian Recovery International[1]

WE HAD SO MUCH DESIRE FOR ONE ANOTHER before we got married, after the honeymoon I was bewildered. I was the one who usually initiated sex—a pattern that continued for two decades. I didn't understand Timothy's disinterest. Now I know he was physically unable—he'd already had sex—just not with me.

After years of my feeling undesirable, Timothy confessed his sexual addiction. Ironically, despite the pain, my feelings were finally validated. "When your alcoholic partner chooses a bottle over you, you can detach. When your partner chooses other sexual partners, the sword cuts deeper."[2]

Now it began to make sense: Timothy felt shameful about sex. The addiction was his *primary* source to meet his needs for love and approval. We are designed for exclusivity, and his addiction excluded me.

Timothy couldn't *risk* initiating sex with me—what if I refused? He had an insatiable need for the approval of women. He falsely believed a refusal would be a devastating statement about his worth.

In many marriages the sexaholic makes excessive sexual demands to prove his worth—to himself. The partner often reacts, "Many co-addicts become sexually 'anorexic' in order to control the addict . . . Often, the more out of control the partner is, the more closed down sexually the co-addict becomes." Dr. Carnes continues, "Sexual anorexia, sadly, speeds up the rhythms of the dance. When she changes clothes out of his sight, he interprets that as a judgment of him and his sexuality. He feels more shameful and wants to escape pain." When their partners enter treatment, a common finding among coaddicts is that they have not had sexual feelings in years. "As soon as they learn that the addict has embraced celibacy as the first stage of the treatment process, they are flooded with sexual feelings. Their sexuality has been on hold as a pawn in the game of addiction."[3]

After years of my feeling rejected sexually, now we couldn't have sex *at all.* Each night as I laid my head on my pillow, I faced reality again. I didn't understand my denial needed to be crucified just as much as Timothy's. Our loving Heavenly Father didn't want us to live the rest of our lives settling for so little of His glory. He wanted to give us the desire of our hearts, but the pain was excruciating while He performed His transforming surgery.

I resented abstinence because it was imposed on me. It was another loss to grieve on the list that kept growing as I learned new information. But as time went on, I started realizing its benefits. "Just as alcoholics abstain from mood-altering chemicals . . . The sex addict, however, has the more difficult job of identifying behaviors."[4] Timothy needed to be sexually sober or celibate to let his feelings surface. He had repressed them his whole life, and the pain they created he medicated with sex. He had to learn how to feel.

It was interesting to learn more about my husband. I enjoyed the closeness we shared. We read recovery books together at night, and I was surprised that abstinence was actually *recommended.* My resentment slowly dissolved as I appreciated its benefits.

In many recovery groups the addict writes a list that defines the behaviors he or she will abstain from as part of recovery. Timothy's list included actions I had no idea were part of his ritual of acting out. For example, female hitchhikers were a major trigger for him. If he saw one, he would circle around several times, deciding if he should pick her up. I learned how hard he worked to avoid eye contact with a hitchhiker now. He had to "abstain" from driving on streets where prostitutes were solicited. He often wanted to be sexual when he felt lonely or hurt. I learned he was vulnerable when he was: hungry, angry, lonely, and tired, or H.A.L.T.

Janice and Jim's Story

"We agreed to be sexually abstinent for four months, and our communication has skyrocketed. Jim's never been much for feelings, but he's getting in touch with some at last."

"Sex was my answer for everything I felt bad about. Now that I can't have it for a while, sometimes I feel like I'm going crazy. But Janice is a good listener, and so are the people in my SA group. When people understand how I feel, the urge to act out gets less, just like they said it would."

"I didn't realize we made love sometimes to avoid conflict. We'd fight and end up having sex without ever resolving the problem."

Jim laughs, "Yeah, I thought, 'What's wrong with that?' but now I know I used sex to escape."

"To learn that life without sex is possible *is* an important part of recovery." Since there can be dramatic healing in relationships with abstinence, it makes sense that "therapists have long recognized celibacy as a strategy for reclaiming sexual feelings . . . Patients . . . start to feel emotions they have not felt for years . . . child abuse memories which have long been repressed often surface."[5]

Couples renew the pleasure of nonsexual touch. Old patterns may be replaced. "For example, some men are always the initiators. Some women never say no. In the recovery process, the rules that formerly governed many aspects of the couple's life together are replaced by new rules."[6]

Overcoming Fears

"Making sex emotionally safe involves coming to terms with the impact of all our previous sexual experiences . . . Every experience of shame about our physical bodies, our sexuality, or our boundaries can impact our current experience of sexuality."[7]

Sheila says, "I regret not going to my own recovery meetings right away. When we were sexual, feelings of inadequacy tormented me. *Will I give him as much pleasure as other, more experienced women?* I competed with the illicit sex he'd engaged in!

"The recovery literature encouraged us to talk about our fears and feelings. I was embarrassed, but I got my courage up. 'Rob, I'm having a hard time. I'm afraid I'm a disappointment to you.'

"Rob said it was all about adrenaline and was only physical. He said he was always afraid of getting caught or catching a disease.

"I need lots of reassurance. The addiction makes me feel so insecure."

Sexual Triggers

Sex was a delicate subject. I struggled with my thoughts of him with other women. I experienced pain, rejection, and even physical repulsion at times.

I was learning the only way to make the feelings go away was to confront them. If they were a quick flash in my mind, sometimes I moved on. But if they lingered, I talked to Timothy about them. I didn't realize at the time they were part of the grieving process. I needed to feel them and grieve them to heal. Instead, I resisted them and often blamed Timothy for them. Later I learned *he*'s not responsible for *my* feelings.

The things that make me feel loved have changed. I feel loved when I see my husband reading his recovery books, when he shares his feelings, when he goes to a recovery meeting. I feel loved when he keeps the checkbook up-to-date and when he's emotionally available to our children. And I feel loved by God that He allowed us to suffer, so that we could be healed.

Restoring Glory to Sexuality

Sex is procreative; God has empowered us with His creative ability! Sex is sacred because it potentially creates new life.

The advent of birth *control* and abortion in the mid-20th century changed the primary purpose of sex in our culture. For the first time we could decide what used to be God's choices. The sacredness of sex began diminishing. Since a child became "wanted" or "unwanted," their numbers diminished in industrialized countries. The value of the unborn baby eroded to the point of legalized abortion the entire nine months of pregnancy in the U.S. What we can control soon evolves into our "right."

Within a relatively short time sex became predominately recreational instead of creational and sacred. We thought we could have sex without the consequences. This mentality saturates our culture, desensitizing us to God's intended purpose of sex.

"They exchanged the truth of God for a lie, and worshiped and served created things rather than the Creator" (Rom. 1:25).

Larry Crabb identifies our only path to freedom, "The cure for sexual addiction and for every form of slavery to something other than God is worship."[8]

As Christians we struggle against powers and principalities of darkness (Eph. 6:12), but we *must struggle*. It's easy to be desensitized; we simply do nothing! The *illusion* of control is now poised to destroy us—body and soul—with our *out-of-control* sexuality.

Sexual addiction takes its toll on Christians because the enemy of our souls has methodically destroyed our *beliefs* about the sanctity of sex. Our denial is just the last domino to fall in an elegant, well-planned trap that promises us freedom from the consequences of sex while it strangles the heart. Recovery is our most effective weapon because it restores our *beliefs* to God's original purpose. The Twelve Steps work because they deal with beliefs as a spiritual issue.

As addicts and coaddicts find freedom from faulty beliefs, shame is replaced with the glory God intended for us. The effects of the Fall are reversed as Christ redeems our sexuality.

The spiritual analogy of our jealous God desiring us only for himself is *glorious*—and attainable—now that shame isn't holding us hostage. Complete intimacy with God spoils us for anything less. Freely giving ourselves to Him and freely receiving His devotion becomes our holy pursuit. In His presence we see ourselves more clearly, allowing our continued healing and wholeness.

chapter 14

REDEMPTIVE COMMUNICATION:
WHAT WE SAY

"The heart of the matter is a matter of the heart."
—Jeff Adams

"Above all else, guard your heart,
for it is the wellspring of life" (Prov. 4:23).

"Real union must ever be in proportion to mutual
truthfulness."—George MacDonald[1]

THE CONDITION OF OUR HEARTS IS FOUNDATIONAL to communication, because our hearts *determine* our words. "For out of the overflow of his heart his mouth speaks" (Luke 6:45).

What fills our hearts overflows into our speech: if it's shame, judgment; if it's resentment, condemnation; if it's joy, gratitude; if it's love, grace. My words came from a needy, insecure heart, and I manipulated others to fill it. I steered conversations, fishing for affirmation; a sense of worth. Of course, only God can satisfy that universal need.

I knew my heart determined my words. The lie I believed was that my heart was healthy. I never questioned it until Timothy's addiction led me into a Twelve Step recovery group. I treated the ailing vital organs of my life with communication workshops, finance seminars, and parenting classes. The skills I learned eased the symptoms, but my shame-filled heart remained unhealthy, and it affected everything.

I couldn't speak healthy words of grace, love, and blessing from a heart overflowing with shame. Communication skills aren't enough to recover the glory and purpose God intended for our hearts.

John Eldredge says, "Caring for our own hearts isn't selfish; it's how we begin to love . . . you can't love well unless your heart is well . . . how you handle your own heart is how you will handle theirs . . . Even though we may try to be merciful toward others while we neglect or beat up ourselves, they can *see* how we treat our own hearts, and they will always feel the treatment will be the same for them. They are right."[2]

I believed in God's salvation, but not in His approval. Scotty Smith expands this concept in his book *Objects of His Affection*. "What is it that causes that *whoosh* sound when you open a new can of coffee? It's the sound of a vacuum sucking in air. Anything that has been vacuum-packed is not simply empty; it is aggressively empty. A vacuum seeks, no, *demands* to be filled, and it is not very discriminating about what fills its hungry void. Vacuum rather than emptiness seems to be a more accurate description of the human heart."[3]

Redemptive Communication: How Jesus Spoke

I like to call the way Jesus spoke *redemptive communication* —words of grace and truth spoken in love. His words weren't powerful because they were delivered with good technique, but because they imparted *life*. "The words I say to you are not just my own. Rather, it is the Father, living in me, who is doing his work" (John 14:10). This verse explains why the communication classes I took couldn't bring peace to my relationships. It's not how we communicate, it's *what* we communicate that makes our speech redemptive. My speech imparted pharisaical standards — especially to me. I prided myself on being truthful, but it wasn't redemptive because there was little grace.

Dr. Henry Cloud states, "Grace and truth together reverse the effects of the fall. Grace, when it is combined with truth, invites *the true self*, the 'me' as I really am, warts and all, into relationship . . . As long as the lying, false self is the one relating to

God, others, and ourselves, then grace and truth cannot heal us."[4]

Twelve Step groups are where I've begun to recover my heart. Most of us don't think we need recovery. That's part of the problem; we're unaware of *what* we need until we have a safe place to talk and realize *what* we feel.

Timothy's addiction forced me down a path I never would have chosen, but it was there I discovered the treasure of *myself*. Brennan Manning says, "The recovery of my true self as the beloved . . . is the goal and purpose of our lives."[5] I suspect I'm just beginning to understand the glory God intended for me.

Nonverbal Communication

Nonverbal cues comprise 93 percent of our total communication.[6] We "hear" instantly what another's posture or facial expression "says." Eye contact is the most effective nonverbal communicator. The first year after Timothy's disclosure, words were simply inadequate. I remember sitting across from Timothy, and we'd look into each other's eyes. Our mouths didn't move, but we said so much. The "conversation" usually ended as tears filled our eyes. Once in a while we'd share a simple thought to confirm we were on the same wavelength. It reminded me of our dating days. Later I read that broken bonds like ours need to repeat the steps of bonding all over again.

To rebuild intimacy and trust we sit close, facing each other. When we have a conversation in bed I gather my pillows and curl up *opposite* Timothy.

I hold his hands, and look into his eyes. It changes everything: it reminds us we're on the same team. We talk awhile—emotional clearance as John Powell calls it. This builds emotional safety to talk about our thoughts and feelings—who we are—which nurtures intimacy.

Dr. Donald M. Joy relates his counsel to Linda, "Do the two of you look into each other's eyes when you are talking to each other?" . . .

"If he looks up, I look away."

"You will have to go back and start over," I told her, "and that could recapture the 'romance' you have lost, too. Think how lonely your husband must feel. It takes only one person to start over again . . . But it will take time, eye contact, and touch. If you are not now looking into his eyes, it means you do not have an honest relationship. Start telling him the truth across the table and look him right in the face while you tell him something like this: 'George, <u>I used to love you so much that I'm spoiled for this world if we can't recapture it again</u>.' The eyes are the window of the soul, and eye contact goes out of any relationship that contains dishonesty in it. Recovery requires a return to honesty"[7]

Try mirroring your partner's body position "Sit or stand in basically the same way as him or her . . . By consciously matching the body position of your partner, you can *consistently* create feelings of acceptance and trust on a subconscious level."[8] Sometimes I'd lie next to Timothy on the bed where he was reading a book, and he looked at me gratefully.

There was so much raw pain during that first year that every movement we made seemed to mean something. An hour later something might trigger my pain and I'd start crying. If he didn't know why, I'd feel rejected and slam the door as I left the room! I'd long for him to come after me in spite of the fact I'd just wounded him . . . and all this was said without any words!

I used nonverbal communication to reach out and to push him away—to affirm him and to punish him. I had so much anger, and only immature ways to express it. I realize now that I sabotaged myself. I wounded him—rendering him unable to listen and understand my pain—which I desperately needed. When he explained that he was now in pain, I often taunted, "Welcome to my world!" This kind of behavior was disrespectful, made me feel worse, and lowered my self-esteem. Worse, it was also shaming, which reinforced the addiction cycle. I had so much to learn!

Eventually we'd untangle the mess: state our feelings, listen to the other, and try to repeat it back to the other's satisfaction. We lost many hours of sleep in the frequent resolution process. I think the entire first year I saw everything in the light of pain. I reacted instead of responding objectively. I don't think our relationship would have survived without the close bond we built the six years before we got married, and, of course, God's unfathomable grace.

Bonding is a powerful ally for relationships. The most important times to bond are when we've been apart. First thing when we awake and the end of the day are opportune moments to look into each others eyes and express sincere interest. This can make us feel intimate the rest of the day.

Our body positions communicate nonverbally: if our body is open, we are emotionally open. Conversely, closed body posture says we're closed to the other. If I cross my arms, I'm saying, "I don't like what I'm hearing." Sometimes I do this to hurt him; our posture and gestures are so *honest*. The hurtful things we "say" with our body language are harder to take responsibility for than our words, but they are just as powerful.

Nonsexual touch says, "I'm here" and "I accept you." The gesture can be as simple as touching feet under a table. It's difficult to blame or attack someone when you're touching him or her. Leaning toward someone is a powerful way to say, "I'm interested." Moving closer encourages him or her that "I'm here and I'm listening." Many of us already use these nonverbal cues, but in a wounded relationship they add much-needed reassurance. Their absence can make a vulnerable spouse feel rejected before a conversation ever begins.

Russell Willingham addresses wives of sex addicts, "As she takes an honest look at her own issues, she usually finds that she, like her husband, was raised in a family environment where legitimate emotional needs were not met . . . Because she was made to believe her childhood needs didn't matter, and she never learned appropriate boundaries, she is out of touch with her present needs. Consequently, she doesn't know how to communicate or address her needs in healthy ways."[9]

Not only was I unaware of my needs, but I felt guilty for having them as well. That's why I blamed Timothy for most of *my* feelings—until I learned about I-messages.

chapter 15

EFFECTIVE COMMUNICATION: HOW WE SAY IT

"Communication is the only avenue to communion."
—John Powell[1]

Verbal Communication: I-Messages

I-messages are nonblaming ways to express a problem *you* have. This simple formula was developed by Dr. Thomas Gordon, founder of Effectiveness Training, Inc.[2] There are three parts:

1. I feel
2. When
3. Because

I feel (feeling word) when (name the behavior) because (behavior or tangible effect).

If your statement creates feelings for your partner, then *he* has a problem and it's his responsibility to state *his* feelings in an I-message: Gary looked up from his mail with a heavy sigh, "*I feel* sad *when* references are made to my addiction *because* I still feel embarrassed to talk about it." However, if Gary wants Gail to listen to this statement, he must *first* reflect her feelings until she feels understood—then she will be emotionally available to listen.

Because most of us are from shame-based families, we tend to take things personally. Negative feelings weren't allowed in Timothy's family. "It could always be worse." "But we have so much to be thankful for." My emotions threaten him, and he gets defensive. To complicate matters, I often do a poor job of I-statements when I'm angry. Then *I* take it personally that he has a problem: "I had a problem first. You need to wait your turn and listen to my feelings instead of expecting me to stuff mine and listen to yours." I-messages are more effective: "*I feel* rejected *when* I'm cut off or ignored *because* my needs and feelings aren't considered important."

Sometimes when I'm tempted to slip into old patterns, I think of my children. "Is this how I would want them to talk to their mates?" That is the reality check that helps me see how much is at stake.

In review:

— The person with a problem makes an I-statement.

— When we realize the person has a problem or feelings, we reflectively listen until he or she feels understood.

— If we have feelings because of his or her statements, we communicate them in an I-message after we've listened.

— The other person now listens to us until we feel understood.

— The process continues back and forth.

I-messages have helped me recognize my feelings and boundaries. When I have trouble thinking of a tangible effect, it is usually because I want to control a situation that doesn't directly affect me. For example, "*I feel* disappointed *when* Jasmine's relatives don't acknowledge her *because?* I'm sad? I feel sorry for her? I'm angry? The fact I can't think of a consequence for *myself* helps me realize this isn't *my* problem at all—there's no tangible effect for me; it's Jasmine's problem. Instead of judging, it would be healthier for me to respect whose problem it is. Since the problem belongs to Jasmine, my *only* role is to reflectively listen: "Jasmine, I thought you might have some feelings about your relatives. I have some time to listen if you want to talk."

For two people to express their feelings takes practice and maturity. It takes self-control to delay the gratification of feeling understood yourself while you listen. Listening is one of the most loving, sacrificial gifts we give others. As codependents we like to "help," so we feel affirmed, which meets our needs, not theirs. When Timothy listens to me, I feel loved.

Usually the present problem is not the one troubling us the most. When we have a chance to express our most accessible feelings, we become aware of the deeper ones. When one offers the gift of listening; the other shares his or her heart, and we are both blessed.

Reflective Listening

Active listening is reflecting back *feelings*—not necessarily words—and the content of the message. If I had to choose only one skill for our relationship, this would be it. When feelings are validated, a person feels understood and can accept his or her feelings and move toward acceptance.

Most of us have rarely seen this modeled or experienced it ourselves. Dysfunctional families want children to be "seen and not heard," so the children learn to feel ashamed of their thoughts and feelings. Christian homes are vulnerable to shutting down negative feelings, "If you can't say anything nice, don't say anything at all," We learn "don't make waves" or "don't rock the boat." These are threats to observe family rules that perpetuate denial and oppression. Freedom of speech is guaranteed by the first amendment, but if we're convinced we don't have anything worth saying, it does us little good. In dysfunctional homes, the only ones free to speak are the parents. Jesus didn't shut people up; He engaged them.

I used to think about how I could offer solutions or help the person—so I could gain his or her approval and keep him or her indebted to me. I knew how to manipulate, but not how to listen.

Gail is dusting the pictures on the piano when she says, "*I feel* sad *when* I see our wedding picture *because* the promises we made have been broken." Notice there is no "you" in the message. This minimizes judgment and helps Gail and Gary take responsibility for their own feelings.

Gary, her husband, needs to validate Gail's feelings of sadness if she is going to feel understood. Active listening reflects back the feelings and the content of the statement, like a mirror: Gary looks up from reading the mail, "Our wedding picture makes you sad." If Gary reflected them accurately, Gail will feel safe to explore her feelings further:

"Yeah, really sad." Gail wipes tears from her eyes.

At this point, Gary realizes Gail wants to talk, so he puts down the mail and walks to the piano, facing her. He looks into her eyes. He doesn't know what to say, but he wants to make her feel better. *But they taught us not to fix feelings, just try to let them know you understand.* "You are terribly sad right now."

Gail collapses into his arms, sobbing. He quietly holds her and lets her cry. In a minute she wipes her tears away and straightens up. "I feel much better. Thank you."

Amazed, Gary goes back to the pile of mail. *This listening thing really works!*

It is that simple and it is that effective. I think <u>one of the most healing aspects of Twelve Step groups isn't that members have an opportunity to talk but that they are listened to, because most of us were not listened to in our families of origin.</u>

This exercise has helped me learn this skill: one of us shares for five minutes and the other *only* reflects the feelings. Since he can't defend himself, I start exploring my responsibility in situations. Potential resentments resolve as I understand *myself.* Then we switch roles. In her book *Codependent No More*, Melody Beattie says "Talking enables us to understand ourselves."[3]

Jonathan Robinson[4] suggests an easy alternative. The listening partner asks, "And what else?" when there is a pause. That is the *only* remark the listening partner can make.

We wanted to know what we felt *before* we repressed it. I didn't want to rage, and Timothy didn't want to act out sexually. We had to get in touch with our feelings. That is when we started active listening without interrupting each other at least 10 minutes every night. We often ended up observing, "I didn't know I felt that way."

It's our responsibility to communicate our needs. Turning squarely in front of Timothy, I take his hands and look into his eyes. "I need you to touch me, look at me, and tell me how I feel. Reflect my feelings back to me." Then I wait. And I pray. I pray that I won't harden my heart, that I won't try to hurt him back for spite, that we will persist until we understand one another—not agree with one another—but understand how each other feels.

Roadblocks to Communication

No one is allowed to correct, judge, fix, give advice, or even praise. These things destroy the emotional safety of the group. People share and everyone else listens. Expressing our feelings verbally is healthy and mature. Having someone listen to them is affirming and healing.

Dr. Thomas Gordon has identified ways we block communication. My personal weakness is reassuring. Our puppy chewed up a pair of earrings my son made me. We only found one of them. I kept repeating, "Don't worry, we'll find it." When I went to bed, he was still upset.

I didn't listen to him! I invalidated his feelings! The next morning I apologized, "I'm so sorry I didn't let you have your feelings last night. If I could do it over I would say, 'You're really disappointed. You worked hard on those beautiful earrings and didn't even get to give them to me.'"

His eyes filled with tears, "I worked for like two hours to make those, Mom." Then he wiped his eyes and asked, "What's for breakfast?"

Roadblocks close our feelings inside us. My son's feelings kept trying to come out, but I kept shutting the door.

Feelings need safety of expression. Picture a turtle that ventures his timid head out of his shell and looks up, blinking. He gathers his courage and speaks. If his feelings are blocked, he pulls back into his shell. If he is encouraged, he continues to explore. "Door openers" encourage others out of their shells; they are phrases like, "Tell me more" or "That sounds interesting." They are the opposite of roadblocks because they invite feelings to come out.

Roadblocks to Communication[5]

1. Ordering (directing, demanding)
2. Warning (threatening)

3. Preaching (moralizing)
4. Fixing (giving advice or solutions)
5. Lecturing (teaching, giving facts)
6. Criticizing (judging, blaming)
7. Praising
8. Ridiculing (name-calling)
9. Analyzing (interpreting)
10. Reassuring (sympathizing)
11. Questioning
12. Diverting (withdrawing, distracting)

It is interesting that Twelve Step fellowships are governed by rules that don't allow roadblocks to occur. We're trying to ensure emotional safety in our family now.

Expressing Anger

Anger is my biggest communication challenge. Dr. Ross Campbell in his wonderful book *How to Really Love Your Teenager* developed a helpful tool: the anger ladder. "Handling anger appropriately and maturely is one of the most difficult lessons in becoming a mature person; one that many adults never learn . . . Each rung on the Anger Ladder represents a progressively better way to express anger. You want to train your teenager to take one step at a time, to go up one rung at a time. How do you do this? . . . be good examples . . . meet him where he is in the handling of his anger and train him from there . . . compliment and praise your teenager in the areas of expressing anger which he did *correctly*."[6]

The Anger Ladder (developed by Dr. Ross Campbell)

1. Pleasant behavior
2. Seeking resolution
3. Focusing anger on source only
4. Holding to the primary complaint
5. Thinking logically and constructively
6. Unpleasant and loud behavior
7. Cursing

8. Displacing anger to sources other than the original
9. Expressing unrelated complaints
10. Throwing objects
11. Destroying property
12. Verbal abuse
13. Emotionally destructive behavior
14. Physical abuse
15. Passive-aggressive behavior

Timothy was at the last rung with his passive-aggressive sex addiction, and I was only two rungs above him with my emotionally destructive raging. We were both babes at expressing our anger! The magnitude of my anger over the infidelity was no match for my immature skills.

Dr. Campbell shared an illustration that could have been Timothy: "Margaret was born and reared in a Christian home. Unfortunately, her parents believed that a child should not be permitted to express anger. So she never learned how to properly handle or resolve it . . . She had one affair after another with married men . . . Until therapy, she could not understand why her lifestyle and behavioral patterns were entirely inconsistent with her basic beliefs."[7]

Passive-aggressive behavior gets back at someone indirectly. It is the opposite of openness and honesty. We use addictions to relieve our pain—*pain that could have been expressed verbally* when it was fear, irritation, frustration, sadness, and so forth. It's a challenge to express feelings we are ashamed of. Now we bounce around on the middle rungs most of the time. The only way to go was up!

Timothy's favorite phrase was, *Don't worry*. In other words, *I don't want you to feel negative emotions*. We had many similar comebacks to our children, all designed to block expression of their feelings: "I don't want to hear any more of that!" Or worse, "Let's pray about it." We were repeating the same messages to our children that we had learned—that had caused us to repress our feelings—that caused us to express anger in unacceptable ways. "I don't want you to *feel*." We said things like that all day long! The oppression of our dysfunctional thinking was exposed.

We learned to validate feelings instead: "Don't worry" was replaced with, "You're worried about something." As we learned to respect feelings in our family, we teased each other when we forgot. We'd say something exaggerated like, "And how does that make you *feel*?" Then we all laughed about it. We raised the consciousness level of feelings and understood how valuable they are.

The High Purpose of Communication

Intimacy is created in marriages and close friendships with the two highest levels of communication: G*ut level* is who I am, especially my feelings and emotions. Occasionally we'll have a *peak communication* experience where we are absolutely honest and open and share a mutual empathy, or communion.[8] Twelve Step fellowships are ideally structured to function at these highest levels of communication.

Dr. Henry Cloud identifies relationship as our greatest need: "Adam and Eve . . . no longer had the fundamental relationship they needed. This thrust them into a state of isolation—from God and from each other. They became people in pain. From this point on, alienation has been our primary problem."[9]

Our deepest need is to reverse the effects of the Fall. To live as God intended, we must recover our true self as His beloved. Communication is the means to restore that relationship with God and others. Our speech blesses others when grace and truth overflow from hearts secure in our own blessedness. This redemptive communication is how we fulfill our glorious calling.

> "A kind voice is to the heart what light is to the eye. It is a light that sings as well as shines."
> —Elihu Burritt[10]

chapter 16

BOUNDARIES

"A good place to start is to insist that her husband get help. But she must stand by her guns and say: 'If you choose not to seek help, I must make some choices of my own.'"—Russell Willingham[1]

"We can cause bad things to happen. This is the law of natural consequences of behavior. If we don't steer our moving car, we will crash."—Dr. Henry Cloud, *Changes That Heal*[2]

I ASKED MY SON, "DO YOU WANT TO TRY OUT YOUR driver's permit?"

He grinned.

Minutes later we cautiously drove down our mountain road. He checked the rearview mirror and his jaw tightened. Another glance, and he sped up.

"You're the one person responsible for your speed, not the car behind you."

He slowed down and his shoulders relaxed. At the next turn-out he pulled over.

I was impressed. There was a time I would've sped up, easily influenced by others. I didn't understand boundaries at all.

Boundaries can be challenging: First, they're invisible; we can't "see" when we step out of bounds, or when others trespass. A boundary is a fence around our area of rights and responsibility. Second, the codependent lies we believe about boundaries are difficult to identify because we grew up thinking they were true.

Twelve Step groups all over the world recite the Serenity Prayer because we need divine help to know the truth:

"God grant me the serenity to accept the things I cannot change, courage to change the things I can. And the wisdom to know the difference" (Reinhold Niebuhr).

Boundaries form early in life. When a child's needs are met, self-respect and worth are internalized. But often boundaries are ignored or even exploited when parents meet their own needs at the child's expense. "Children who have been taught their lessons by having love turned on and off eventually conclude that their sole worth and goodness lie in their ability to fulfill the needs and wishes of others. In no sense do they live *for themselves* but only *for others*."[3] The result is a society where many of us don't know who we are responsible for. Healthy boundaries mean *we* take responsibility for *ourselves*—and *only* for ourselves.

I was first introduced to boundaries in Jane Nelson's parenting books. I learned that parents should speak as respectfully to their children as they do to their best friends.[4] I'd trespassed their boundaries without realizing it. But the worst thing was—they didn't realize it either—ignoring boundaries was normal in our dysfunctional home.

Since values are learned from modeling, I parented the way I was parented. The fences intended to protect individual personalities in our family were unrecognizable. I was determined to change.

It helped me to visualize boundaries by comparing them to driving. We stay on our side and communicate changes with signals. We can't control an oncoming car, so we don't try. If we don't like how someone else drives, we don't force our way into that person's car and take over his or her steering wheel; we are detached in a healthy way. When the rules of the road are violated, collisions can occur, causing injury.

In this chapter the examples of driving appear exaggerated and ridiculous, but that's the point: our ignorance and violations of our own boundaries are preposterous at times.

Denial

Ray Ann is cooking breakfast when Jerry enters the kitchen. "You got home so late last night."

"Yeah, I thought the meeting would never end. Then I was hungry, and I had to get gas . . ."

Ray Ann feels a familiar twinge of fear, but ignores it; the possibilities—well, she doesn't want to go there. Because she chooses denial—*she* is experiencing the consequences of *his* behavior. He should be the uncomfortable one, but she is. Even though Ray Ann is passive, she's made a choice about *her* boundaries: <u>her apparent lack of concern lets him off the hook</u>. <u>If she remains silent, she enables his behavior.</u>

In other words, a car slips on the icy road but the warning goes unheeded by the driver. Taking the next turn too fast, he sideswipes a car, but keeps driving.

His wife grips the door handle, her knuckles white. *Was that my imagination, or did he hit that car? He's not acting like he hit it, so I'm probably wrong.*

She *chooses* to believe his denial is valid. *Our* boundaries are about *our* choices, whether or not we realize it.

Ray Ann never saw her mother confront her alcoholic father. She is a coaddict, because she enables her husband's addiction. When she sees a flagman ahead on the road, she ignores his stop sign, just like her mother taught her. Coaddicts usually choose spouses who also ignore the flagman.

I am a lot like Ray Ann. I ignored reality. I believed if I confronted Timothy he would think I didn't trust him. Duh!

Blame

Linda sensed a distance with John. *Ever since his class reunion he's been withdrawn.*

She was devastated when she discovered John's affair with his high school sweetheart. *Is this is my fault? I'm getting older— and heavier. Maybe I don't satisfy him anymore.*

John was unsympathetic, "You haven't had any time for me since you started that class."

"I know, and I'm so sorry. I feel awful about my weight too."

"I didn't want to say anything, but now that you mention it—"

"I can change. I'll diet."

The car keeps speed with the driver's anger. His wife has caused so many of *his* problems! The car careens out of control and smashes into a tree. Blood spurts from an ugly gash near his temple. Unaware of his peril, he ignores the pool of blood pumping from his head. John turns toward his wife who is barely conscious, "I'm so mad at you! That's why we hit the tree!"

"It's all right. I can get the car fixed."

When we blame others, we aren't taking responsibility for our behavior. When others blame us, they aren't taking responsibility for their behavior.

If we are easily convinced *we* are responsible for the choices *others* make, then *we'll* feel obligated to experience the consequences of *their* choices. We may even think we are making godly sacrifices when *we* endure *their* consequences, but we are only enabling their unhealthy behavior.

Drawing the Line

Randy and Tina clung to each other, their shoulders shaking with sobs. "I feel so bad. I won't ever do it again. I don't know why I did it in the first place."

"I don't either, but I forgive you."

"I don't—I don't deserve it."

"I love you. We'll get help and figure it out."

"No, I'm sure it won't happen again. This is it."

"This is a big deal. I think we need some help, with our pastor or a counselor."

"Well, it's in the past now. I could never face going to church again if our pastor finds out. God's always helped us before. I'm sure we'll be fine."

Tina went to their pastor in spite of Randy's embarrassment. "You're taking responsibility for yourself, which puts you in God's hands instead of Randy's. So you'll be all right no matter what."

"I know, but I'm sad."

"Of course you are. I hope he'll agree to counseling soon. There's no reason to believe he won't repeat his behavior if he doesn't face the cause."

"I was afraid of that. Maybe this wasn't even the first time."

"I'd like you to consider what his consequences should be if he doesn't get help."

Tina spent more time in God's presence. She filled her journal with letters written to her Heavenly Father, and what she sensed were His responses. She'd heard the word "detachment" before; *I think that's what I'm doing. I'm not desperate for Randy to meet my needs anymore. When I'm upset, I think of praying instead of calling him.* She learned to depend on God rather than her husband for her worth and purpose. Her self-acceptance blossomed.

She was sad Randy wasn't growing too. He needed so much affirmation and still refused counseling. She didn't trust him.

Tina called her closest friends and group members to garner the emotional support she needed. "If Randy continues to refuse help, I'm going to ask him to move out. I love him and would miss him, but I'd be dishonest, expose myself to disease, and set a poor example for my children. I won't do that."

"Well, I admire your strength. I don't know if I could do it."

"It's taken me some time. At first I couldn't even think about a separation."

"What's changed?"

"I'm learning how God sees me, and I feel better about myself. I like who He made me to be. I'd be sad without Randy, but I'd be all right."

It's foggy on the highway as the two cars approach. Randy

drifts into the oncoming lane. The cars collide head-on; everyone suffers major injuries. A witness dials 911. Randy turns to his wife, "I don't think we need to go to the emergency room. We're not hurt that badly." He's lost a lot of blood by the time the paramedics arrive, but insists he doesn't need medical attention. "Tina, we'll be all right. I promise I won't ever have another accident again. I'd be so humiliated if we went to the emergency room."

Tina gratefully allows the EMT to start an IV and prepare her for transport.

Many of us don't seek counseling or a support group until we're in critical condition *and* our husbands agree to it. We stick Band-Aids on gaping wounds and wonder why our relationships are bleeding to death.

A counselor asked me why I never sought counseling for myself. *I had no idea.* "Ultimately, in marriage, spouses give up a lot of 'you' and 'I' freedoms in order to create a 'we.'"[5] We needed a "you" and an "I," but all we had was a codependent "we."

Identity theft is considered a crime in this technological age, but our enemy has robbed God's children of their true identities since life began in the garden, and he has perfected it.

Gail's Spiritual Immaturity

Gail walks into the den and notices Dan is watching an X-rated video. "How can you watch that stuff?"

"I'm not hurting anybody. It'd probably do you good to sit down and watch it with me. It couldn't hurt us in the bedroom."

"Do you really think so?"

"Yeah, I do."

Could he be right? She was a new Christian and was learning about submitting to her husband.

Dan is driving on the wrong side of the road. Gail feels uneasy, "I think something's wrong."

His confidence and convincing arguments reassure her.

When Dan gets sleepy he pulls over so Gail can drive. She buckles her safety belt, looks both ways, and pulls out onto the wrong side of the road.

God never intended for wives to submit to immorality. Eph. 5:22 needs to be taken in the context of the surrounding verses: "Husbands, love your wives, just as Christ loved the church and gave himself up for her" (Eph. 5:25). The husband is called to give his life for his beloved—demonstrating the *mutual* submission intended in marriage—an analogy of Christ and His Bride, the Church. The goal of our submission is holiness, never compromise.

Her First Boundary

John told Linda, "I made an appointment at the health department to get tested for STDs."

"Thank you. I want to abstain until you get your results back."

"That's only fair."

Linda felt relieved and proud of herself. *That wasn't so hard.*

Linda realizes John is drunk as he fumbles in his pocket for the keys. She's risked her life before, afraid if she said anything she'd offend him, or worse, lose him. *Not this time.* "John, I'm driving home." Her voice was confident, and he walked to the passenger door. Linda was learning who she was. To allow herself to be a victim of John's denial would violate her newly discovered boundaries.

Our Boundaries Are Our Responsibility

"*He* was the driver," or "It's *his* problem," rationalizes *our* denial. If his behavior is violating our boundaries, then it's our responsibility to take action.

Jesus said, "First take the plank out of your eye, and then you will see clearly to remove the speck from your brother's eye"

(Luke 6:42). He gave us the responsibility to change *first*. Enforcing our boundaries is a powerful form of communication. We can't change our partner, but we can love him enough to get our point across: "I have appealed to our relationship and to the possible hurt you are going to cause. But if this is not enough, I will start removing things in our relationship that you want and value. I don't want to, but if that's what it takes for you to take responsibility for your problem, I'm willing to."

It is the utmost challenge to detach from our partner's sexaholic behavior. We would be more objective if their escape was alcohol; but when they numb their pain being sexual with someone else—either real or imagined in fantasy or pornography— it's hard not to take it personally. We have to make support groups and time in God's presence our highest priority. Grace and truth are our best friends.

Steve Arterburn, cofounder of the Minirth Meier Family Life Clinics, describes sex addiction this way:

"The addict races faster and faster down the avenue of addiction. He convinces himself that he is in control, that he can stop any time he wants. But by the time he truly sees the need to stop, he realizes he is in a runaway vehicle with no brakes. Only when he runs head-on into something immovable—the law, a disease, public humiliation—does he come crashing to a halt.

"And yet, it does not *have* to be this way. There is another avenue the addict, and his loved ones, can take. It is called *recovery*."[6]

MY HUSBAND'S STORY

I WANT TO SHARE A LITTLE OF MY STORY WITH YOU in order to help you understand that we sexually addicted husbands have certain defects of character that keep us in bondage. We are skilled liars and deceivers, and we will say and do anything to keep the access to our drug protected. We think that without it we will die. We think that we are only truly alive when we act out—even though we are dead inside as soon as the act is over and looking forward to the next fix—the one that might finally work for us. We are convinced there is no way out of the lifestyle we have chosen and that we will be stuck in it until we die.

We attempt to deceive those closest to us and cover up our secret by being loving and caring. In fact, the majority of us will work in caring professions—teaching, ministry, or medicine. Our caring often leads us to even more resentment—which, of course, we are not prepared to deal with in healthy ways—and our resentments add more fuel to our addictive fires. We are without hope of escaping the web that we have created for ourselves.

I was married to Molly when I was 20. She was my high school sweetheart. I compulsively masturbated through high school and remember thinking the night before my wedding "this will be the end of that." However, since I had been using sex to hide from my feelings for many years, this pattern became stronger with the inevitable conflicts and feelings that came with marriage.

I was raised in a family that did not allow the expression of feelings or strong emotion. Consequently, I didn't learn to deal with my feelings in a healthy way—I buried them until they came out in sexual fantasy and acting out. My father died when

I was 10 years old, and my mother overmothered me in an attempt to make up for my father's absence. This all led to my overwhelming need for the approval of others in general and approval from women in particular. I look back now and see that the beginnings of my acting out in my marriage coincided with feelings of disapproval and unhappiness in Molly that I simply could not deal with.

I spent most of the next 20 years living a double life. At home I attempted to be the most loving and giving husband possible. This was motivated by my intense shame and guilt about my secret life. I would act out, feel horribly sorry, and then tell myself I would never do it again. Then I would come home and try to be a super husband, dad, and Christian man. Inevitably, resentment followed when Molly was unhappy about something. How could she not recognize what a super person I was? Soon the resentments and desire to hurt back led to the next acting out activity. Of course, to me, all of these reasons were a mystery; I only knew the pull of the addiction to find the next fix. All of these patterns were there, just hidden by layers and layers of denial.

I always told myself that if I ever contracted an STD, I would confess to Molly. After 20 years of acting out, that is exactly what happened; I finally brought everything out into the open. When Molly forgave me, I felt so free and happy—elated really—that I was not going to have to carry the burden of maintaining the lie. However, reality soon struck; at last I felt free, while Molly suffered under the burden of dealing with the pain and sorrow caused by my lies, deceptions, and repeated unfaithfulness. This was a very hard time—she couldn't understand why I was so happy—and I struggled to understand why she was so sad.

Looking back, I see that Molly carried the far heavier load in the beginning of recovery. She had to deal with the loss of all that she thought was true in our relationship, the pain of betrayal, the fear of disease, the difficulty of forgiving unlimited numbers of indiscretions, and facing her coaddiction. During this time she also had to be mom to our large family, maintain our home, and deal with a husband who was incapable of understanding her feelings of grief and loss. I see her tremendous burden now as I look back with the experience of recovery. I wish I had understood and appreciated her pain and burden at the time, but I didn't. I was generally relieved and happy to be free of the addiction.

I began attending Twelve Step groups, and we became involved with a church that supported recovery. I slowly made progress in admitting my powerlessness over the addiction and finding some peace and sanity. I began to have a healthier view of myself. However, the focus was all on me as the addict; our counselor assured us that Molly was "absolutely not codependent!" Through this experience I learned that it is critical to find a counselor that understands addictions in general and is experienced in sex addiction in particular.

I had about five years of sanity and freedom from bondage during this time. We renewed our vows and our marriage grew stronger with the real me being involved for the first time. When I assumed I was strong enough, I stopped attending Twelve Step support groups. I could do this on my own now.

Tragically, my son's ex-girlfriend committed suicide in our home. I chose to deal with the pain by moving back into my addiction—I chose secrets and darkness again—rather than staying in the light. Even though I was surrounded by caring and loving friends, I believed the lie that my sex addiction was the only real way to deal with my pain—or to not deal with it. Now I understand that as an addict I deal with pain by addicting; the bigger the pain in my life, the more I will tend to addict.

I acted out for four years! Unfortunately, we addicts don't start over—we start where we left off—always looking for more to get the same level of fix. I went back to living the double life, this time knowing for sure I was stuck forever.

As I look back at this time, I see evidences of the toll my addiction had on my life. Because of my shame and guilt, I never had confidence in my abilities or talents in any job—ever. I was always afraid that somehow my bosses or coworkers would find out about the real me and I would be exposed for the horrible person I was. This led to financial loss from not being a whole person at work. There was also the wasted hours cruising, money I spent acting out, and the extra money spent to make up to my wife and family for it.

Finally there is the addict's golden promise: Maybe if I move, change careers, start a new business, or get more education I will not have to act out again. I tried all of these things! Wherever we moved and whatever I did, I took myself with me, and the addiction was part of me.

After four years, the guilt and shame took their toll; I was so mean and awful that Molly finally told me to get some help or move out. She thought I was depressed, but I knew what the problem was—again.

The counselor insisted I confess to Molly that I was acting out sexually. She recommended a Christian ministry specifically for sex addicts. I began counseling and attending support groups there. Molly also attended a spouses' group. I had one year of sexual sobriety with this ministry.

I can't remember what caused me to slip, but I began to act out again. I lied to my groups; I lied to my counselor; I lied to Molly; and I lied to myself. I returned to my addiction in spite of the help and support provided by this ministry. If I had been honest, it would have worked for me, but I wasn't. I let it be external help and counsel, not the inner, self-motivated work that I'd done previously in a Twelve Step program. I acted out for two more years.

When Molly felt prompted to write this book, she was unaware of my true state. I remember intense shame because of my acting out during this time. *What if Molly's book gets published and I'm caught acting out?* In spite of that fear, I didn't think I'd be able to quit the addiction.

Then one night Molly said, "You know what my expectations are?"

"What?"

"That someday I'll learn you're acting out again, just like the last two times."

I didn't know what to say. *Should I tell her?*

"I'd rather have one day of honesty than a lifetime together with deception."

"Do you really mean that?"

"Yes, I do."

"Well, then, I've been acting out again, Molly."

Now she didn't know what to say.

"You said you'd rather have one day of honesty, so I'm taking you up on it."

She found her voice, "You're serious, aren't you?"

At that point in our 32-year marriage, she had received only about 6 years of truth and honesty compared to 26 years of lies and deceptions.

Until four days ago I had seven months of sobriety and sanity. Then I did something that triggered Molly's grief—I turned the stove off. She cried for five hours. I couldn't stand it—I felt judged, and I wanted to get even—so I ate three big breakfasts at McDonalds— trying to find some comfort. I let her feelings define me; I internalized them as disapproval.

We talked about it for two hours. She felt invisible—like she didn't matter—when I turned the stove off without asking her. Her overreaction was actually a result of the grief she suffered as a young girl when she felt she didn't matter. Logic didn't change my feelings of disapproval. That night, I went to a massage parlor; I wanted to hurt her for expressing her feelings and get some comfort for my own hurt. I immediately confessed it to her.

For the first time, I recognized how much power I allow Molly's approval or disapproval to have over me. It wasn't her—it was all me—my shame reacting personally to her feelings. I learned I am fully responsible for my own reactions; I can't blame Molly or anyone else for them. I must take action by getting the professional help I need to stop acting out in passive-aggressive ways. I want to learn how to deal with Molly's strong feelings in healthy ways. Otherwise, it is only a matter of time until I begin looking for unhealthy ways to numb the pain. Only by finding freedom from my approval dependencies and accepting myself will I be released from the addictive activities I have used in the past.

A word that means a lot to me now is *regret*. After 26 years of acting out, all addiction has left me with is *regret*. <u>In spite of its empty promises of pleasure and escape, in the end, I'm left with sorrow and regret.</u> I share this word now because it keeps me sane today—knowing that the only thing I will have to show for another slip is regret.

chapter 18

A FAMILY DISEASE

"A single recovery can serve as a leaven for change in
an entire family."—Dr. Patrick Carnes[1]

"BECAUSE ADDICTIONS ARE CONSIDERED a family dis-
ease, recovery is most effective if it involves the whole family."[2]

A friend asked me, "Don't you worry about what your husband's sex addiction could do to your kids?"

"I used to; but it's just the opposite: our home is emotionally
safer now than it was before. We talk about *everything*. We're
open about our own shortcomings, so the kids feel accepted in
spite of their shortcomings."

This hasn't always been the case. The first 15 years we parented as our dysfunctional families of origin had—control, manipulation by guilt, invalidating their feelings—the typical authoritarian home where children were to be seen and not heard
or "I'll give you something to cry about." At that time, we barely
had a relationship with our oldest teenagers.

Like our parents before us and their parents before them, we
assumed we were healthy. Denial allowed us to look at our respectable appearance—and no further. We were professionals;
we lived in a nice house, and we were active in church. Until
the addiction came to light, we thought we were a normal, happy family, *exactly* like the families we grew up in. We didn't
know *that* was the problem.

Dr. Patrick Carnes calls children from dysfunctional, disen-
gaged, rigid homes the *vulnerable* children. "They are not bad
children, but rather children in pain who seek relief. They will
use 'highs' to feel better—food, sex, TV, whatever it takes to

numb the pain."[3] Our two oldest "numbed" their behaviors. Their overeating, premarital sex, and drug abuse baffled us until we understood the addictive system *and* how dysfunctional our home was. Before they moved out, we had several years to correct our mistakes, and the behavior improved dramatically.

The parenting classes and books focused on *skills*, but our recovery groups focused on *beliefs*. Treating our children respectfully improved relationships, but the shame-based beliefs oppressed *our entire family*. We were stunted Christians with enough faith for salvation but not enough to believe we are deeply loved and cherished; we compensated by gaining everyone's approval, especially God's. This was the family tradition we passed on to our children—until the addiction forced us into recovery.

The most loving—and most painful—thing God has done for me is expose my dysfunctional beliefs. Our invisible prison with bars of shame was condemned. Demolition began when it was exposed to the light, out in the open. It lost its power to oppress the next generation—our precious children.

> ### "If we don't talk about it, then it's *not* an okay subject." —Dan Gerald, *Holy Scars*[4]

After 10 years in recovery, our counselor suggested we tell our oldest kids about the addiction. "Their world needs to make sense to them," she said. Timothy and I were no longer blaming each other; we were both committed to our personal recoveries and wouldn't persuade the kids to take sides. This was an important decision we made together with our counselor.

Ask yourself the following questions *before* the decision is made to tell young adult children:

- Are they emotionally stable?
- How do they handle anger?
- Do they have a good support system? (friends, youth pastor)
- Are there other adults they can process their feelings with?

- Are they mature enough to respect appropriate confidentiality?
- Do we have enough self-acceptance to risk them telling others?
- What do we expect to accomplish by telling them?
- Can we accept their painful feelings without judging them and reflectively listen?
- Are we prepared to let them grieve their losses?
- How much information should we share? What would God consider appropriate and helpful?
- Do we have a counselor who can help them work through their feelings?
- How many appointments should we make for them?

One addiction specialist writes, "Couples who are recovering together have had to work out their own guidelines. Because of the sensitive nature of sex, a lot seems to depend on the age of the children. Most . . . have chosen to openly talk to their teenagers, but not to younger children . . . It is best to wait to talk with our children until . . . we can handle the situation if others find out about it."[5]

Timothy took our two oldest sons, 21 and 23, out for lunch. He explained sexual addiction and apologized, taking full responsibility for his behavior. The oldest said, "We thought Mom was mean, and Dad was the nice guy. This explains a lot; Mom is really strong."

The two boys confessed their own sexual struggles. To my relief, they were minor. For the first time in 22 years we were honest with our kids. Timothy didn't go into details, but he didn't whitewash his behavior either. We now enjoy an open and honest relationship.

During the next 4 years, Timothy relapsed into his addiction. I didn't realize what was happening, and we fought a lot—but I didn't know why. Timothy finally confessed, and we addressed the real problem. Meanwhile, it was time to tell the next three children.

They have yet to meet any other children of sex addicts, so they carry a lonely burden. Statistically, however, they unknowingly interact with hundreds of them at school. Guarding the knowledge of sexual addiction in the family places them in a vulnerable position where they may feel ashamed or different, *separate* from other kids. John Eldredge warns, *"You must not go alone. From the beginning, right there in Eden, the enemy's strategy has relied upon a simple aim: divide and conquer. Get them isolated and take them out."*[6]

Since it would help our kids to learn from the experiences of others, I asked them if they would share their experiences.

The following chapters contain their stories. We hope they will help others identify their feelings, realize they are not alone, and encourage honesty and acceptance within families.

Our children are in various stages of the grief process. Our oldest was influenced the most by our dysfunction, and he emphasized how much we worked. Dr. Carnes notes that dysfunctional families don't play very much. I remember how I struggled when he was young; I'd grit my teeth when I saw him playing Legos *because he wasn't working*, which was *my* means of approval. Now I play with my kids—not out of duty—but because my values have changed. I'm much happier!

Sharing our stories is an invitation to honesty and acceptance, countering our dysfunctional family rules. "Covering up the family secret is very much a part of the disease of addiction . . . Being open with our children is part of *our* recovery; allowing them to share with whomever they want is part of *their* recovery."[7]

We only get one opportunity to tell our kids.

Insights from pastors and counselors are invaluable, because it's hard to be objective in our closest relationships. Confession can bring healing, trust, and intimacy if we humbly take responsibility for our behavior and surrender our loved ones' reactions and grief process to God.

The purpose of sharing my children's stories is to promote open communication within families. Focus on your children's feelings after you tell them. Sometime later, so they won't feel discounted, you may ask them to read the following chapters. There are questions online for you to discuss *together*. Communication is not optional in a healthy family. *Honesty* is the most effective means to change a family's dysfunctional beliefs. When we talk to our children openly about our own shortcomings, they feel acceptable in spite of theirs.

Confessing the sexual addiction to our children is our greatest opportunity as parents to overcome our dysfunctional beliefs, perpetuated by *shame*, and overcome them with *grace and truth*.

OUR DAUGHTERS' STORIES

Erika's Story, age 14

If you could take back the past, would you? Imagine for a second what life would be like without pain. Who would you be? Do you think you would be happier? If you do, I want you to know I disagree with you. Why? Because you must stand in the deepest shadow to see the clearest light. And often through wrong's own darkness we see the weary strength of right. Those who have not known sorrow cannot know the infinite peace that falls on the troubled spirit when it sees—at last—release.

I am young and know nothing of the pain you have endured, but I do know pain. Everybody does. I feel it when my parents are fighting, when my mom is crying. It comes to me when I think of the past, what I lost, and the ways I have been used. It comes to me, I'm ashamed to say, when I look back on the old me. Pain is universal.

I remember when my mom first told me, she had gotten off the phone with Dad and was crying. As I sat next to her, trying to comfort her, she told me. She said my dad was a sex addict and that he had only told her 12 years ago when I was a baby. Out of their 32-year marriage it took him 20 years to tell her. When she told me, it didn't hit me as hard as I would have thought. I don't think I even realized what she meant.

I had known, even before she told me, that my dad was a sex addict. I pieced it together from their fighting. I was only 12, but looking back I can see it affected my life in many ways. It affected me more than I still probably know. I was very emotional and mean. The anger I felt toward my parents I took out on my friends at school and my little brothers. I also took it out on myself. I believed I was fat; I hid diet books under my bed and was terribly self-conscious. I remember at school I didn't even want to walk to the bathroom by myself.

If I had a choice of how I would find out about my dad, it would be my mom telling me before I pieced it together from their fighting. Figuring out something like that and trying to deal with it alone is hard. I think I just pushed it away. I stuffed it down. I didn't like the thought that my dad, my hero, the best guy on the earth, was like that.

I hated it when they fought. Sometimes I hated them. At times I locked myself in my room, trying to get away from it and trying not to deal with it. I remember late at night not being able to sleep because of the yelling in the room next to mine. It was terrible. Eventually, God gave me grace to handle and forgive. They fight less now, and I feel so much more open with them. Before, I felt very alone and misunderstood by my parents. You may have to look hard to see that those who have hurt you the most are the ones you should be most thankful for. My dad is still my hero because he has done one of the hardest things there is to do, open up and tell the truth, even if it means putting yourself in the lowest pit ever.

Still, growing up with a sex addict dad makes life at school very hard, especially when it gets around. When I was in the eighth grade a girl who was an old friend was told about my dad and that my mom was writing a book on it. She told all my friends, and I was devastated. I came home crying. I would become a reject, my dad's job could be in jeopardy, and it seemed all my friends were going to be talking about me behind my back. Well, things didn't turn out bad at all. My old friend and I talked it out and are still friends. Her friends didn't tell anyone else, and no rumor was started.

Life is still really hard. I often grieve. I grieve for my mom—the pain, lies, and deceit she has had to deal with. I grieve for me, and I grieve for my brothers. I love my parents so much, when I see them hurting, it hurts me. Yet, when my mom falls apart and talks to me about her feelings and what she's dealing with, I feel closer to her. Being open with your kids forms even deeper love, trust, and respect. In a family, everybody gets hurt when something like this happens. There's no way around it.

One thing I grieve for most is the thought that my parents have considered divorce. I cry at the thought of it. If my parents divorced, the result would be terrible. Having to choose one love over the other isn't right. That's the worst thing you can do to a child who's hurting. Your child may look back and remember fighting, but at least he or she remembers parents together.

So, if you could take back all the pain and hurt from the past, would you? Would I? With all of my heart—no, I wouldn't. In fact, I am thankful for my dad's addiction. I love my dad, and I am so proud of him for how much he's grown already. I love my mom so much for the pain she has endured and all that she's gone through. I love who I am; what I've gone through has shaped me into somebody I'm proud of. I have forgiven those who hurt me and caused me pain. And I want you to see you are not alone.

I ask you—if you have not, think about how your kids feel about this. I encourage you to talk to them and tell them that, with God, this becomes bearable. Support them and try to understand what they are going through. It helps me so much that my mom often likes the music I like; just simple things like that can mean so much. Give your kids time. Hearts can be mended. They may become scarred, but they can be mended with the love and grace of God.

Kelly's Story, age 22

I found out about my dad's addiction my junior year in college. I came home from my waitressing job late one night during Christmas break and was playfully arguing with my younger brother in the kitchen. My mom came in and started to scream at us. I sighed with annoyance; I was tired from a long day and unwilling to get yelled at over what I perceived as having fun. Normally I would listen and apologize, but this time I did not. I defended myself, and so did my brother. My mom stopped crying and looked at my dad who had now entered the kitchen and said, "We have to tell them."

My brother and I perked up; my imagination was racing with a thousand thoughts that seemed to revolve around the sudden insecurity that one statement could make you feel. *Tell us what?* What could they possibly tell us that would explain her erratic behavior, behavior we had come to know as normal? I felt like the hardwood floor beneath me had turned to sand.

My parents brought us into their bedroom. I felt awkward, and I knew everyone else felt the same. We were all sprawled across their bed with a box of Kleenex between us. My dad's voice shook as his eyes welled up with tears. He said he hadn't been completely honest with us and he had really hurt my mom. He said more, but I don't remember it.

I do, however, remember how I felt; I was shocked. I felt like I had been slapped across the face. The life I thought our family lived had been nothing but an illusion. I had grown up with others complimenting me on how wonderful my dad was and how I was so lucky to have someone like him as a father. My friends often told me they wanted to marry someone as sweet as my father. I agreed it would be hard to find someone as great as him. I felt betrayed at his words, but worse, I knew I felt only a little of the betrayal my mother had to cope with.

I tried to play strong and tell my dad that it was OK and that we love him. I told him that a study conducted at my Christian university found that more than half of the guys looked up porn on the Internet. I would have said anything to show him that we weren't going to reject him. I was scared to react because I knew they had stepped out on a limb to tell us. I looked around the bedroom at everyone internalizing his words and trying to rationalize what they were hearing. I couldn't help but smile in awkward nervousness, and felt horrible for it. I wanted to laugh at the absurdity of life, but I didn't.

I can't overemphasize how grateful I was that they finally decided to tell us. Their truthfulness explained much of my child-hood. I always knew something wasn't quite right at home, but I had no idea what it was.

I considered my dad a workaholic. While I was at home he was immersed in his small business and traveled frequently. My mom became an increasingly independent, strong figure for the family. She, however, always seemed to have some sort of outlet to channel her pain. While I was in junior high, it was garden-ing. During high school, it morphed into an antiquing addic-tion. It was like parts of her were wise beyond her years and parts were like a child, reaching out for something—anything. I re-spected her but couldn't explain her. Learning the truth helped answer those questions I had. I finally had the pieces to make sense of the puzzle. It's only when the puzzle is put together that one can begin healing.

Later that same year, I was preparing to travel abroad to work against sex trafficking. I was talking to my mom on the phone and found out the extent of my dad's sex addiction; I was shocked to hear that he actually visited prostitutes. Maybe I didn't want to know. Most daughters do not want to hear the words *Dad* and *sex* in the same sentence.

That next morning I went to class and was still in shock. I didn't want to be at school, but I didn't want to be home be-cause then I would think about it. I was standing with my arms crossed, in a daze, when my teacher came up to me and said, "You're standing in a defensive pose. How are you feeling to-day?" I looked at her, and my eyes welled up with tears. She hugged me close to her, and I said I had found out something about my dad that was kind of upsetting to me. She questioned me, "Sex addict?" I felt like I was betraying him to say anything, but I didn't have to because my face told all. I asked her how I could go to the other side of the world to work against sex traf-ficking. I felt like I would be working against my dad. Later that day she had the class pray for me. Although the students didn't know what they were praying for, their support and love wrapped around me and touched the deep isolation I felt. I was reminded that the Body of Christ is called to bear one another's burdens in love. These brothers and sisters did more than any of them knew that day.

While I believe my dad had a choice—and he chose poorly—I can see how God really does work everything for good for those who love Him. Knowing about my dad's addiction actually helped deepen my understanding of the complexity of social issues while I was abroad. I frequented a particular café and watched foreign men pick up the local prostitutes. My heart was often heavy with the burden I felt, not for the prostitute or the man, but for the state of our sinful world. Knowing about my dad helped me have a deeper sense of compassion because I love my dad unconditionally and I realized that God called me to love others unconditionally too, even if that figure took the form of my enemy. I was continually reminded that the line between good and evil runs between each of us, and that these men also had an image of God within them. Most of all, I was reminded of the life of Jesus and that He came for both of them equally. My father's addiction helped me better comprehend the depths of the grace of Christ.

As the child of a sex addict, I think the path of healing can be especially difficult because juggling the whole gamut of emotions at times feels overwhelming. There are feelings of anger, rejection, isolation, neglect, and feeling unimportant. Sex addiction isn't socially acceptable. It's awkward and uncomfortable to talk about with parents. I felt sadness and pity for my mom—maybe even bewildered about why she chose to stay with him, but at the same time I felt love and compassion and a genuine desire for them to work it out.

I have come to believe that true healing is doing something with the knowledge we have gained. I don't believe it's OK to just move on with my life. But it isn't healthy to become fixated. There is something that awakens the spirit when we touch others with the raw wisdom, pain, and grief of our past experiences that makes us who we are.

chapter 20

OUR SONS' STORIES

Gabriel's Story, age 16

I don't like feelings, because feelings hurt. No one likes to feel pain, but we do, and everyone deals with feelings in different ways. One of the many feelings I have is anger. This feeling is easily accessible for me and is how I react to many circumstances.

When my parents brought us all together and told us about my father's sexual addiction, I went blank. I felt like a plain brick in a wall of a million plain bricks. I'm sure now that I was confused, but I didn't realize that immediately. I remember saying with soggy eyes that I was angry, which I was, but that wasn't all I felt. When it comes down to it, I was confused. I didn't know what I was feeling or what I should be feeling. I did know that I felt alone; my siblings had clearly defined feelings they understood. I didn't.

It introduced a trust issue; my dad had been the one I had turned to most when I was hurt. My dad would hug me and ask me what was wrong or just comfort me. I rarely turned to my mother with my feelings when I had a choice, because it felt like she was emotionally unstable or upset all of the time. When my dad told us the truth, I used his deceiving as an excuse to not communicate my feelings fully. When my parents asked me later how I felt, I gave short, mumbled answers and slowly buried my feelings.

I finally cracked. My mother asked me how I was feeling. My reply was something like, "What does it matter?" My parents then told me that I had to share my feelings with them. I became angry and told them I had buried my feelings, and I didn't need or want them. My dad then explained to me that my anger was not discarded; it was a part of me. It would come out and show itself in different ways if I did not deal with it correctly and talk it to death, which is the healthiest way. I dealt with my anger then. I try now to always talk about my feelings so that I don't exert them in unhealthy ways.

I know that my family and I have learned and grown a lot through the pain and hurting, and I can express my feelings better now.

James's Story, age 19

The first time I found out about my father's sexual addiction I was 15 years old, a freshman in high school. My parents took my older sister, my younger brother, my younger sister, and me and brought us all into their bedroom to tell us that Dad had been unfaithful to Mom. He had struggled with pornography, strip clubs, and had slept with other women. It was hard to take. As I sat there, my former image of my father was shattered. I felt deeply sad and betrayed, but at the same time I felt gladness in my heart. I was glad because my dad stood up, he was open enough to confess to us, and this told me that he really did want to change.

Suddenly, I understood the deeper problem that lay behind my parents' fighting. Knowing that they had already been through the ordeal once before, most of my fears were laid to rest about them getting a divorce. Their attitude was one of wanting and hoping to solve the problem . . . not letting the problem tear apart their marriage and the family.

I didn't feel too affected by all this, surprisingly. As time went on, things went back to normal; I forgave my father because I knew he really wanted to change, and I saw the same willingness to forgive in my mother.

In the following years, money became scarce. I worked at an after-school job my junior year to help pay for my gas and other needs, despite having a very busy schedule. My senior year in high school, I found out that my dad had fallen into his old habits again. My heart broke. It was a whole different situation this time around. An old wound that had started to heal had been reopened, but deeper this time. My feelings of betrayal went the deepest, because I realized that all the times I had gone without or had to pay for things with my own, limited money, my dad was spending money on his addiction. I felt like my dad loved his addiction more than me. When they told us about the addiction this time, I still gave my dad a hug and said that I forgave him, but in my heart that was not the case.

My anger toward my dad started appearing in everyday situations. Mostly, I think, through disrespect. Anytime he asked me to do something, I wouldn't want to do it. I found myself avoiding him and not trusting him. Finally, my dad took me aside and told me that he felt hurt by me. He could feel my anger toward him. I was forced to examine my feelings and my actions, and I was surprised at what I found.

I hadn't forgiven my father for betraying me. I didn't feel he was "worthy of forgiveness." The effect of this was that I had come to blame him for all my problems. I blamed him for everything from money problems to my own sin. Once I realized that I was placing all my responsibility on him, I could consciously separate what he was actually responsible for from what I was responsible for.

I realized that, more than anything, I was scared of myself. I was scared because I realized how easily sin could lead to the problems that Mom and Dad faced in their marriage. I was scared because I knew I was sinful, and I knew how easily I could do the same thing my dad did.

The key in the whole process was God reminding me of His great grace. I could forgive my dad only when I realized that he deserved forgiveness just as much as I did. His sin was great, but so was mine. If I condemned my father, then I would have to stand in judgment as well. God made it known that His saving grace stands over both of us. God is saving my father, and God is saving me.

Thank you, God.

Preston's Story, age 24

First and foremost, I love my father with all my heart. I think the world of him and, yes, he is a good father and a great man. He is well-respected, loved, and looked up to by those who know him.

My dad struggles with a very common problem that usually ends up destroying families: He is addicted to sex. When you hear that you may think, "Well, who isn't?" But the truth is sex addicts struggle with sex on an unhealthy level, putting sex before their loved ones and their families.

Being the son of a sex addict is hard on a lot of levels. At first, you don't believe there is a problem, and then you find out how serious the problem is. You feel maybe it's your fault or your mom's fault. It's hard to point a finger at someone you love—especially the one with the problem.

I didn't know about my father's addiction when I grew up, but I saw the effects it had on my family. My mom was often sad or angry, and my brothers and sisters and I didn't quite know the reason.

My father has had this problem since he was a teenager. He finally told my brother and me at a restaurant one day. I was 22 years old with a family of my own already. The truth was hard to swallow, but my love for my dad never changed. Instead, I felt sad for him. To live a lie must have been hard. At the same time, I understood a lot of my parents' old arguments and fights that never used to make sense.

My mother truly cares about her family to stay with my father after finding out about his adultery. The truth is, we all care about him so much that we have to believe he can change. We need to believe there is hope for him.

I have struggled with pornography to the point of causing marital problems. Sometimes it's hard not to question whether these problems of mine were passed down from my father somehow. But I believe every man is tempted with these things on an almost-daily basis. I know that hiding things from your wife does *not* work. I am a firm believer that, "The truth shall set you free." I believe that if everything is out in the open, it's a better way to live. It breaks the cycle of guilt and makes a husband and wife a *team*. The problems can be worked on together.

It's easier for me to relate to my father's addiction because I was addicted on a lower level myself. It doesn't mean he doesn't love me when he does these things, it means he has a problem resisting temptation.

Jeff's Story, age 26

I always thought it was normal for my dad to work long hours. After all, being the oldest of the kids is not the easiest situation to be in. I had a lot of responsibilities, like watching the younger kids, getting the baby to sleep, laundry, dishes, mowing the lawn, homework, work for Grandpa, house cleanup, and big projects like home renovations and building fences. It was pretty hectic, but we still managed to have dinner every night as a family, which was wonderful.

A lot of the time my dad was not there, but Mom told us he was working late. We were all grateful that he provided us with so much: food, shelter, and cool vacations. He even built me a skateboard ramp. My dad is an awesome dad. He was gone a lot of the time, but I never thought something was wrong. Since our family worked hard on weekly chores, it was natural to think he was working hard to make money for us.

I will never know what nights he was out cheating on his wife. That is what hurts the most; we ate dinner as a family every night, yet he would go out cruising the streets, looking for women to have sex with at night. It makes me feel very betrayed.

It's not like my dad was a mean or overbearing father. He is the best dad I've ever met. I'm still proud to be his son and still thankful he's my dad. I remember the awesome good times we've had over the years. From talking to my dad you would never know he had been unfaithful to his wife. You would never guess he could be a sex addict or pick up hookers or be unfaithful. Period.

We never had a clue anything was amiss in the family. We never heard him leave at night. We thought he was out working late in his office. We had no reason to doubt him; why would we? He never lied to us about anything else.

I guess where I'm going with this is that when I found out my dad was a sex addict I was in shock for months. I am 26 and live in Las Vegas and will soon be married. My wife-to-be has three kids from her previous marriage, and I love them so much. I decided I didn't want to be gone as much as my dad. I want to always be around—not just for dinner. I always put them first and work second. I won't stay out late working when I could be hanging out with them. Kids grow up fast. I don't want them to miss me like I missed my dad a lot of the time. Before I found out about my dad's addiction, I had already made steps to correct the small shortcomings I saw in my father. I decided that even if I make less money and don't have as many things, I want to be home more.

After the shock wore off, everything kind of made sense. I remember taking a trip to Florida with my dad. It was awesome to be alone with him, and we had some really fun father-son times together. I walked the beaches or went to theme parks by myself during the day while he attended seminars for his business. I noticed some stuff missing out of my suitcase. I had some jewelry wrapped up. One night it was missing and I thought maybe the housekeeper took it. The stuff that was stolen was very important to me; it belonged to my ex-girlfriend who committed suicide. They were irreplaceable and precious things that were stolen from me.

When he told us about the addiction, I thought that some woman was with my dad in our hotel room and took them from my bag. Whether it's the truth or not, it's hard to know it's even a possibility.

Honestly, the weirdest part of having a sex-addict dad is wondering when or how he satisfied his urges. But I really don't want to know the details.

I am sad that my wonderful dad's image is changed now. He was amazing; he never drank or did drugs, but made healthy choices. He always did the right thing in hard situations. All of us kids had this awesome image of our dad. Meanwhile, almost all of our friends' parents were getting divorces, turning into alcoholics, secretly drinking, or whatever. It's really hard to find out years later that he was unfaithful and lusting after other women; especially when you have such a beautiful image of your father.

A lot of feelings are involved: betrayal, anger, resentment, distrust, disgust, and hurt. It feels as though something was wrong with all of us that he couldn't just hang out and play video games or watch movies with us.

His issues must have been really deep and very severe. It's unthinkably tragic that my dad pulled the wool over our eyes for so many years. I still love my dad, and I always will. Our relationship changed at first, but now I have worked through my feelings toward him. I feel grateful that he finally told us what was really going on. I'm happy that he is trying to be honest and confront his issues instead of hiding them.

I am grateful that he and my mom are still together. They are working through forgiving one another and go to meetings for sex addiction. As other people going through the same problems read this, I hope they'll realize healing is possible through honesty and solid relationships with your kids.

OUR GLORIOUS CALLING

"Praised be the grandeur of the God who can endure to make and see His children suffer." —George MacDonald[1]

BY THE TIME THE SEXUAL VIOLATION ran its course, nothing looked familiar; we scarcely recognized our own lives. We didn't know what to do, but we *didn't* expect to hear this: your healing will be grounded in admitting your own addictions and defects.

What? We knew our marriage was in crisis, but we didn't realize our identity was too. We were shocked to discover how unhealthy our spouses were, but assumed we were fine. Then we each asked ourselves, "If my partner is a sex addict, then *who am I?*"

We began this journey against our will, betrayed by our partner. We finish it with a far different identity: no matter what our spouses do—or anyone else—we are the beloved of God. We are uniquely created in His image and bear His glory. We've been invited into the Garden of Gethsemane to share the sufferings of Christ. There we found the understanding we needed from one who also suffered unjustly. As our hearts slowly emptied themselves of excruciating grief, we healed. Eventually we realized Jesus had to redeem us as well as our partners, but just as much for *us*. We recognized our true state—acceptable only because of God's grace—like *all* humanity.

This revelation empowers us to forgive our offenders—and it allows us to forgive *ourselves*. Our shame is healed as the truth replaces the lies of our faulty beliefs. Our failures don't matter to God; He anticipates them. We no longer have to prove our worth to ourselves or others: it is defined by God. We are startled by the glory He intended for us! Our identity as His beloved determined more than our healing—it redefined our lives. We can now be fully alive as we reflect His glory.

God didn't betray us after all; He was drawing us to himself to reveal our glorious calling. Gratitude replaces sorrow as He brings redemption from betrayal. He exposed idols we didn't even realize had taken us captive. Now we can worship Him as never before—as He originally intended—and satisfy the deepest longings of our hearts.

For years, Ps. 13 expressed my anguish: "How long must I wrestle with my thoughts and every day have sorrow in my heart?" (v. 2). I was afraid the last two verses would never apply to me, but now I read them with gratitude: "I trust in your unfailing love; my heart rejoices in your salvation. I will sing to the LORD, for he has been good to me" (vv. 5-6).

Jesus showed "the full extent of his love" by humbling himself as a servant to wash His disciples' feet. His identity wasn't threatened *because* He knew who He was: "Jesus knew that the Father had put all things under his power, and that he had come from God and was returning to God" (John 13:3).

Like Jesus, we also have to know *who we are* to humbly exemplify His character: Shame, lowly tasks, fear of rejection, or betrayal by our spouses don't have to threaten our identities. Unfaithfulness was a painful price to pay for this lesson, but it was worth every tear.

A Redemptive Community

"We are never stronger than when we are open about our brokenness."—Roger Thoman, Pastor

We are now able to take our places in God's healing community, *not in spite of* this trial, but *because* of it. We won't pass off another's pain with trite platitudes. We will look beyond someone's behavior to his or her pain-filled heart. We've changed—we accepted our broken state—and cast ourselves fully at the mercy of God. He then revealed our true identities—His beloved—and

He endeared himself to us as never before. Now we have received the grace that allows us to mercifully accept others.

Larry Crabb writes, "When life kicks us in the stomach, we want someone to be with us as we are, not as he or she wishes us to be. We don't want someone trying to make us feel better. That effort, no matter how well intended, creates a pressure that adds to our distress."[3]

Henri Nouwen says, "Consolation is a beautiful word. It means 'to be' (con-) 'with the lonely one' (solus.) . . . To console does not mean to take away the pain, but rather to be there and say, 'You are not alone, I am with you.'"[4]

A comment I often hear from people who attend Twelve Step groups is, "Isn't *this* what church is supposed to be like? I wish this is what my church was like." We *long* for acceptance, understanding, and affirmation.

"One of the most important things we can do with our secrets is to share them in a safe place with people we trust . . . Bringing our secrets into the light creates community and inner healing. As a result of sharing secrets, not only will others love us better but we will love ourselves more fully."[5]

Larry Crabb concludes his insightful book *Shattered Dreams* with these words: "We're new creations whose core identity is no longer sinner but saint . . . I envision a revolution that creates a community of broken people united not by their problems or diagnoses but by their hunger for God. I envision a revolution that frees people to fully participate in that community because they feel the safety of the gospel that embraces people rather than judges them, that joins hurting folks more than advises them on how to feel better, that supernaturally equips people to pour life into one another."[6]

That sounds a lot like my recovery group.

John Eldredge concurs: "A true community is something you'll have to fight for. You'll have to fight to get one, and you'll have to fight to keep it afloat. But you fight for it as you bail out a life raft during a storm at sea. You want this thing to work. You *need* this thing to work . . . This *is* the church; this is all you have. Without it, you'll go down. Or back to captivity."[7]

Lazarus' Recovery

The sisters sent word to Jesus, "Lord, the one you love is sick" (John 11:3).

I bid you, come, Lord Jesus. You love me, and those I love; I am powerless over this disease.

"When he heard this, Jesus said, 'This sickness will not end in death. No, it is for God's glory so that God's Son may be glorified through it.' Jesus loved Martha and her sister and Lazarus. Yet . . . he stayed where he was two more days" (vv. 4-6).

God, I don't understand your timing. I don't like it, and I want to control it.

"'Lord,' Martha said to Jesus, 'if you had been here, my brother would not have died'" (v. 21).

"When Mary reached the place where Jesus was and saw him, she fell at his feet and said, 'Lord, if you had been here, my brother would not have died'" (v. 32).

Lord, if you are God, how come my husband has this addiction?

Lord, if you're my protector, why have I been betrayed?

"When Jesus saw her weeping, and the Jews who had come along with her also weeping, he was deeply moved in spirit and troubled. 'Where have you laid him?' he asked.

"'Come and see, Lord,' they replied.

"Jesus wept" (vv. 33-35).

Jesus, you've wept with me. You share my sorrow.

You don't just know how I feel, you feel how I feel.

"Then the Jews said, 'See how he loved him!'" (v. 36).

See how Jesus loves our husbands!

"'Take away the stone,' he said" (vv. 38-39).

They assumed Jesus came to mourn his friend's death, until this moment.

"'But, Lord,' said Martha, the sister of the dead man, 'by this time there is a bad odor, for he has been there four days'" (v. 39).

Lord, please don't expose my husband's addiction. It's repulsive! Can't we keep it hidden? Everyone will be offended!

"Then Jesus said, 'Did I not tell you that if you believed, you would see the glory of God?'" (v. 40).

Lord, how can you be glorified in this terrible situation?

"So they took away the stone" (v. 41).

People are going to find out the truth. How will they react? We're about to reveal our worst secrets.

Is the price of healing worth the humility of the truth?

"Jesus called in a loud voice, '"Lazarus, come out!"'" (v. 43).

He called my husband's name!

He wants him to come out of his dark captivity to meet Him in the light.

"The dead man came out, his hands and feet wrapped with strips of linen, and a cloth around his face. Jesus said to them, 'Take off the grave clothes and let him go'" (v. 44).

He couldn't free himself and Jesus didn't ask him to.

Others unbound Lazarus, just like in our support groups: our shame is removed as we share our stories and find unconditional acceptance.

Jesus invited us to share His suffering in the Garden of Gethsemane. In John 11:40 He invites us to share His glory: "Did I not tell you that if you believed, you would see the glory of God?"

RESOURCES

Call the national headquarters for a local contact phone number in your area to find meeting times and locations:

S-Anon International Family Groups (S-Anon)
P.O. Box 111242
Nashville, TN 37222-1242
615-833-3152
E-mail: sanon@sanon.org
Web site: http:/www.sanon.org

Codependents of Sex Addicts National Service Organization (COSA NSO)
P.O. Box 14537
Minneapolis, MN 55414
763-537-6904
E-mail: newhopenserenity@yahoo.com
Web site: http://www.cosa-recovery.org

Recovering Couples Anonymous (RCA)
P.O. Box 11872
St. Louis, MO 63105
314-830-2600

Prodigals International (www.iprodigals.com)
6619 132 Ave. N.E./PMB 262
Kirkland, WA 98033-8627
Offer curricula for establishing recovery ministries for addiction and coaddiction; excellent info on web site.

National Association for Christian Recovery (NACR)
P.O. Box 215
Brea, CA 92822-0215
714-529-6227
Web site: http://www.christianrecovery.com
E-mail: hopehappens@earthlink.net
Publishes online library and STEPS newsletter.

The Christian Alliance for Sexual Recovery
P.O. Box 2124
Tupelo, MS 38803-2124
601-844-5128
Dr. Mark Laaser, author of *Faithful and True* offers sexual addiction recovery workshops.

New Life Ministries
P.O.Box 866997
Plano, TX 75086
1-800-639-5433
www.newlife.com
Steve Arterburn, founder

BASIC SUPPORT GROUP GUIDELINES

1. We are here *only* to listen to one another. While one person is sharing, we ask the group to simply be present and attentive with no feedback or cross talk. We are here to give and receive support. Fixing, giving advice, or offering solutions is disrespectful and can make a person feel inadequate and judged. Our goal is emotional safety and trust.

2. There will be an opportunity for each person in the group to talk if he or she feels comfortable. If you would rather not, simply say, "I pass."

3. Listen with your heart to understand how others feel. Many of us were never listened to in our families. We will learn from the insights of others.

4. Give others permission to be where they are in their growth process. Our only expectations are honesty and faith in God's ability to heal us.

5. Do not interrupt, distract, or encourage those who move into painful feelings such as grief, guilt, or sorrow. It's *their* turn to explore *their* feelings, even if we find it uncomfortable. When each group member finishes sharing, it's encouraging for the others to say, "Thanks for sharing."

6. We are committed to confidentiality. Whatever is shared in the group is not to be shared outside of it. Trust is a gift we give each other.

7. We read these rules at the beginning of every meeting so we don't repeat the dysfunctional behavior many of us learned in our families.

REFERENCES

Title Page

1. Patrick Carnes, *Out of the Shadows* (Center City, Minn.: Hazelden Educational Materials, 1992), xi.

Introduction

1. Marnie Feree, "Women and Sexual Addiction," taken from her workshops at Woodmont Hills Counseling Center, Nashville <www.woodmont .org>. Audiotapes, article available from Prodigals International <www.iprodi gals.com>.

2. "Recovery from Sexual Addiction: An Interview with Mark Laaser" Online library of the National Association for Christian Recovery (NACR), <http://www.christianrecovery.com>.

3. John Eldredge, *Waking the Dead* (Nashville: Thomas Nelson, 2003).

4. Russell Willingham, *Breaking Free* (Downers Grove, Ill.: InterVarsity Press, 1999), 206.

Chapter 1

1. Steve Arterburn, *Addicted to "Love"* (Ann Arbor, Mich.: Servant Publications, 1996), 208.

Chapter 3

1. Eldredge, *Waking the Dead*, 200.

2. "The F Word: Forgiveness and Its Imitations: An Interview with David Augsburger," STEPS interview by Lela Weaver 10-3-2003, Online library of the National Association for Christian Recovery (NACR), <http://www.chris tianrecovery.com>

3. Dietrich Bonhoeffer, *The Cost of Discipleship* (New York: Macmillan Co., 1967).

Chapter 4

1. Willingham, *Breaking Free*, 2.

2. Donald M. Joy, *Bonding: Relationships in the Image of God* (Waco, Tex.: Word Books, 1985), 78.

3. Ibid., 80.

4. Marsha Means, *Living with Your Husband's Secret Wars* (Grand Rapids: Fleming H. Revell, 1999), 124-25.

Chapter 5

1. George MacDonald, *Happy Thoughts* (New York: James Pott & Co., 1894), 19.

2. Henry Cloud, *Changes That Heal* (Grand Rapids: Zondervan, 1990), 157.

3. Larry Crabb, *Shattered Dreams* (Colorado Springs, Colo.: Waterbrook Press, 2001), 125.

4. Andrew Murray, *Abide in Christ* (Fort Washington, Pa.: Christian Literature Crusade, 1997), 67-68.

Chapter 6

1. Cloud, *Changes That Heal*, 103.

2. Patrick A. Means, *Men's Secret Wars* (Grand Rapids: Fleming H. Revell, 1999), 27-28.

3. John Powell, *The Secret of Staying in Love* (Allen, Tex.: Tabor Publishing, 1979), 5.

Chapter 7

1. Brenda Ueland, *If You Want to Write* (St. Paul, Minn.: Greywolf Press, 1938), 23-24.

2. Merle Fossom and Marilyn Mason, *Facing Shame* (New York: W. W. Norton and Company, 1986), 123.

3. "Stats & Facts" online resource. Prodigals International, 6619 132nd Ave. N.E., PMB 262, Kirkland, WA 98033-8627, <www.info@iprodigals.com>.

4. Patrick Carnes, *Don't Call It Love* (New York: Bantam Books, 1991), 146.

5. Carnes, *Out of the Shadows*, 6.

6. Jennifer Schneider, *Back from Betrayal* (Center City, Minn.: Hazelden Educational Materials, 1988), 83.

7. Carnes, *Out of the Shadows*, 9.

8. Means, *Men's Secret Wars*, 213.

9. Arterburn, *Addicted to "Love,"* 28.

10. Means, *Men's Secret Wars*, 170.

11. John Powell, *why am I afraid to tell you who I am?* (Argus, Ill.: Argus Communications, 1969), 74.

12. Powell, *The Secret of Staying in Love*, 8.

13. Means, *Men's Secret Wars*, 128.

14. Ibid., 129.

15. Charlotte Davis Kasl, *Women, Sex, and Addiction* (New York: Ticknor and Fields, 1989), 113.

Chapter 8

1. Gerald G. May, *Addiction and Grace* (San Francisco: Harper Collins, 1990), chapter 1.

2. Brennan Manning, *Abba's Child* (Colorado Springs, Colo.: NavPress, 1994), 74.

3. Means, *Men's Secret Wars*, 80.

4. Patrick Carnes, *Contrary to Love* (Minneapolis, Minn.: CompCare Publishers, 1989), 137.

5. Carnes, *Don't Call It Love*, 152.

6. Carnes, *Contrary to Love*, 146.

7. Patrick Carnes, *Silent Shame: The Path to Addiction* (Minneapolis, Minn.: The Gentle Press, 1990).

8. Cecil Murphey, *Invading the Privacy of God* (Ann Arbor, Mich.: Servant Publications, Vine Books, 1997), 10.

9. Schneider, *Back from Betrayal*, 46.

10. Willingham, *Breaking Free*, 204.

11. Carnes, *Don't Call It Love*, 145.

12. Carnes, *Contrary to Love*, 137.

13. Schneider, *Back from Betrayal*, 46.

14. Ibid., 26.

15. Carnes, *Don't Call It Love*, 359.

Chapter 9

1. Willingham, *Breaking Free*, 128.

2. Shannon Ethridge, *Every Woman's Battle* (Colorado Springs, Colo.: Waterbrook Press, 2003), 62-64.

3. Murray, *Abide in Christ*, 22.

4. MacDonald, *Happy Thoughts*, 40.

5. Powell, *The Secret of Staying in Love*, 22.

6. Gertrude Chandler Warner, *The Boxcar Children* (Chicago: Albert Whitman & Company, 1971).

Chapter 10

1. Carnes, *Contrary to Love*, 152.

2. Carnes, *Don't Call It Love*, 356-57.

3. Carnes, *Out of the Shadows*, 144.

4. Melody Beattie, *Codependent No More* (Center City, Minn.: Hazelden Educational Center, 1992), 185.

5. Carnes, *Out of the Shadows*, 131.

6. Cloud, *Changes That Heal*, 80.

7. Carnes, *Out of the Shadows*, 143.

8. Carnes, *Don't Call It Love*, 365.

Chapter 11

1. Manning, *Abba's Child*, 131.

2. Cloud, *Changes That Heal*, 28.

3. Marnie Feree, "Women and Sexual Addiction."

4. Russell Willingham, director, New Creation Ministries (NCM), P.O. Box 5451, Fresno, CA 93755 (559-227-1066; e-mail: newcretionmins@aol.com).

5. David Peck, M.F.C.C., director, Aesthetic View Institute, 2350 W. Shaw Ave., Suite 118, Fresno, CA 93711.

6. Henri Nouwen, *Bread for the Journey*. Daily Meditation "Being Safe Places for Others" (New York: Harper Collins, 1997).

Chapter 12

1. American Social Health Association (ASHA), P.O. Box 13827, Research Triangle, NC 27709-3827. Pamphlets: What you need to know about STDs and Condoms, Contraception, and STDs.

2. Willingham, *Breaking Free*, 200.

Chapter 13

1. "Safe Sex" article by Dale Ryan, online library of the National Association for Christian Recovery (NACR) @ <http://www.christianrecovery.com>.

2. Carnes, *Don't Call It Love*, 161.

3. Ibid., 165.

4. Ibid., 244.

5. Schneider, *Back from Betrayal*, 234.

6. Ibid., 242.

7. Ryan, "Safe Sex."

8. Crabb, *Shattered Dreams*, 121, 129.

Chapter 14

1. MacDonald, *Happy Thoughts*, 122.

2. Eldredge, *Waking the Dead*, 211-12.

3. Scotty Smith, *Objects of His Affection* (West Monroe, La.: Howard Publishing Co., 2001), 75.

4. Cloud, *Changes That Heal*, 25, 27.

5. Manning, *Abba's Child*, 125.

6. Jonathan Robinson, *Communication for Couples* (New York: MJF Books, 1997), 19.

7. Joy, *Bonding: Relationships in the Image of God*, 77.

8. Robinson, *Communication for Couples*, 20.

9. Willingham, *Breaking Free*, 204-5.

Chapter 15

1. Powell, *why am I afraid?* 47.

2. Dr. Thomas Gordon, *P.E.T. in Action* (Wyden Books, U.S.A., 1976), 85.

3. Beattie, *Codependent No More*, 184.

4. Robinson, *Communication for Couples*, 43.

5. Gordon, *P.E.T. in Action*, 31-32.

6. Ross Campbell, *How to Really Love Your Teenager* (Colorado Springs, Colo.: Chariot Victor Publishing, 1993), 73-74.

7. Ibid., 70-71.

8. Powell, *why am I afraid?* 54-63.

9. Henry Cloud, *Changes That Heal*, 50.

10. O. S. Hoffman, *Optimistic Voices* (Battle Creek, Mich.: O. S. Hoffman, 1908), back cover.

Chapter 16

1. Willingham, *Breaking Free*, 200.

2. Cloud, *Changes That Heal*, 100.

3. Powell, *The Secret of Staying in Love*, 12.

4. Jane Nelson and Lynn Lott, *I'm On Your Side* (Rocklin, Calif.: Prima Publishing and Communications, 1990).

5. Henry Cloud and John Townsend, *Boundaries Face to Face* (Grand Rapids: Zondervan, 2003), 192.

6. Arterburn, *Addicted to "Love,"* 214.

Chapter 18

1. Carnes, *Don't Call It Love*, 329.

2. Schneider, *Back from Betrayal*, 267.

3. Carnes, *Don't Call It Love*, 137.

4. Focus on the Family interview with Dan Gerald, pastor from Anchorage, Alaska, and author of *Holy Scars*.

5. Schneider, *Back from Betrayal*, 267.

6. Eldredge, *Waking the Dead*, 187.

7. Murphey, *Invading the Privacy of God*, 10.

Chapter 21

1. MacDonald, *Happy Thoughts*, 132.

2. Crabb, *Shattered Dreams*, 185-86.

3. Nouwen, Daily Meditation, "Giving and Receiving Consolation."

4. Ibid., "Bringing Our Secrets into the Light."

5. Crabb, *Shattered Dreams*, 186.

6. Eldredge, *Waking the Dead*, 199.

FREE
Small-group discussion starters available at
www.beaconhillbooks.com

Contact the author at:
mollyannmiller@uno.com

Young adults who would like to be directed to online
discussion groups may contact the author.